Punta Cana, Dominican Republic.

Travel and Tourism Guide

Author

Wyatt Harris

·

Published
By
InformationSource.
16192 Coastal Highway Lewes,
DE 19958. USA.

.

Table of Content

ABOUT PUNTA CANA CITY 1

INTRODUCTION 1
THE HISTORY 6
Culture 18
TRAVEL GUIDE 20
Climate, Weather and when to Go 26
Health and Safety 29
Electricity 36
Health 40
Things to Do 44
Overview of the Area 44
Dominican Cigars 49
Golf in Punta Cana 54
Nightlife 57
Off the Beaten Path 61
Reserva Ecologica Ojos Indigenas 63
Segway EcoTour 68
Shopping 69
Dining 85
Wedding 97
Sports and Activities 103
Places with Free Wifi (OffResort) 122
Rums 125
School Visits 128
Hotels in Punta Cana 130
Apartments 133
Stanza Mare, Bavaro Beach, Dvr 133
Presidential Suites Punta Cana 135
Terraza Art Villa Dominicana Punta Cana 137
The Sanctuary @ Los Corales Apartment Punta Cana .. 139
Punta Cana Bavaro Suites Pool 141
Everything Punta Cana Los Corales Apartment 143
Exclusive Residencial Nautilus Bavaro Punta Cana 145
Monkey Banana Bavaro Punta Cana Apartment 146
Villa Blanca Punta Cana 148

Villas.. 150
    Deluxe Villas Bavaro Beach & Spa 150
    La Flor Del Caribe Villa Punta Cana............................... 151
    Villas Paseo Del Sol Punta Cana.................................... 153
    Beach Villas & Apartments Larimar Punta Cana........... 155
    Alex Villas Golf Resort Iberostate 156
    Resort Atlantic Villas & Spa Punta Cana 158
    Tropical Villas Deluxe Beach & Spa Punta Cana............ 160
    Villa Cocotal Palma Real Punta Cana 161
    Beach Resort Caribbean White Sand & Ocean Punta Cana
    163
Hotels... 164
    Iberostar Punta Cana Hotel 164
    Hotel Riu Bambu Punta Cana... 166
    Riu Palace Bavaro Hotel Punta Cana 168
    Grand Sirenis Punta Cana Resort & Aquagames........... 169
    Barcelo Bavaro Palace All Inclusive (Adults Only)......... 172
    Riu Naiboa Hotel Punta Cana 174
    Bahia Principe Grand Aquamarine (Adults Only).......... 175
    Riu Palace Macao (Adults Only) Hotel Punta Cana 177
    Four Points By Sheraton Hotel Punta Cana 179
Resorts 181
    Barcelo Bavaro Palace All Inclusive Punta Cana 181
    Impressive Punta Cana Hotel... 182
    Sanctuary Cap Cana, AllInclusive Adult Resort 184
    Barcelo Bavaro Beach (Adults Only) Hotel Punta Cana 186
    Grand Palladium Punta Cana Resort & Spa 188
    Majestic Elegance Punta Cana (Adults Only) Hotel 190
    Dreams Punta Cana Hotel.. 192
Holiday homes 194
    V&V Beach House.. 194
    Green Village 03 Punta Cana 195
    Hotel El Conde De Villa Rosa Punta Cana 197
    Town House 36B, Punta Cana Village 199
    Punta Cana Family Home... 200
    Costa Hermosa B102 Hotel Punta Cana........................ 201
    Villa Diane Punta Cana.. 203
    Corte Sea D302 Hotel Punta Cana 204
    Villa Cocotal 206B Punta Cana....................................... 206

Bungalow In Cap Cana Caribbean Hotel Punta Cana 207
Economy hotels 208
Hotel Plaza Jireh Punta Cana 208
Coconuts Hotel Punta Cana 209
SunAdventureTravel Hotel Punta Cana 210

About Punta Cana City
Introduction

Punta Cana is the region located at the furthest eastern point of the Dominican Republic. This traveler's paradise is known for its gorgeous white sand beaches, its luxurious resorts, and its tropical vibe. Visitors can scuba dive, go deep sea fishing, swim with dolphins, or go horseback riding in Punta Cana, all under a cloudless sky and surrounded by sparkling blue waters. There are also plenty of cultural options in the Dominican Republic, where visitors can tour classic Dominican homes, try traditional food or drinks, or tour some of the production facilities where products like cocoa, cigars, rum, and coffee are made. Hours/availability may have changed.

The sugary sand of a Punta Cana beach is so soft, so perfectly golden that you might think it was synthetic. And in fact, in this easternmost tip of the Dominican Republic, it's possible. By definition, Punta Cana is a manufactured Caribbean getaway, completely catering to the needs of sunseeking vacationers who enjoy allinclusive resorts but care little about venturing away from their hotel. Boasting more than 24,000 hotel rooms at affordable rates, Punta Cana beckons to jetsetters, especially the budgetminded kind.

While this destination is better known for relaxation than adventure, visitors can get their fill of thrills hiking to Hoyo Azul or taking on challenging golf courses like Punta Espada or La Cana. Overall, this reasonably priced, Caribbean hideout is made for travelers of all ages seeking a relaxing turn from the norm.

Everything in this place, from the international airport, the roof of which is covered with palm branches and bamboo, is infused of the Dominican culture and architecture's originality. The last stands in the same style, most hotels of Punta Cana have the same roof. Features of this type of construction indicate that the state controls the construction of the resort, so as not to disturb the natural appearance of the spot. The basic styles of architecture: Spanish Colonial, and the rustic style of the brightly painted farms. Hotels are successfully entered in the fabulous scenery of palm forests and local environment.

They meet a variety of guests from all over the world.

This beautiful resort is inspired with Dominican culture, and stands out an eclectic mix of Spanish, Mexican and Dominican cultures in the architecture, design and art, cuisine and traditions. Literature and Fine Arts for a long time have been imitating the European style directions. And only in the middle of the 19th century there were prerequisites for the creation of original works relating to their own tradition and modernity. In the cities in Dominican Republic appear cultural institutions and open independent theaters, galleries and literary societies. Music and dance are at the heart of this culture. The most popular form is the meringue, a kind of rumba. Popular type of music is bakata.

Most vacationers choose allinclusive Punta Cana hotels. This system will save you from unnecessary worries at the resort. There is no need to take the remaining money by the end of rest, and worry about the huge bills at the restaurant as you have already paid for everything. An additional set of service is always present, and at each of the accommodations it is different. There are also common economyclass hotels, where you can stay for the limited budget. Young companies, and sometimes families prefer such hotels. In such places, there is no organized system of food for guests, but often in or near there are institutions in which vacationers can have a cheap snack. All the hotels are comfortable, modern and have the necessary facilities.

We offer 1402 hotels in Punta Cana Dominican Republic with low rates and discounts. Our reservation system provides cheap and luxury hotels in Punta Cana, hostels, motels, B&B and other budget accommodation in Punta Cana. We have excellent hotel deals in central Punta Cana. You can also book Punta Cana airport hotels at low prices. Our system is secure and absolutely chargefree.

The History

Punta Cana is today a popular resort area in the Dominican Republic, located on the far eastern point of the country in the province of Altagracia and is one of the Caribbean's most popular resort areas. Most of the tourists who come to the area are unaware that Punta Cana is not specifically the name of the whole area to the south of the airport where the very first hotel was built.

In fact, although the East Coast of the Dominican Republic is frequently referred to as Punta Cana, it actually encompasses several areas: (Cap Cana, Punta Cana, Cabeza de Toro, Bavaro, El Cortecito, Arena Gorda, Macao and Uvero Alto). Most of today's resorts and hotels are located in Cabeza de Toro, Bavaro, Cortecito, Arena Gorda, Macao and Uvero Alto, but nearly all of them use the name "Punta Cana" in their branding even when they are not geographically located in Punta Cana.

Origin

In 1969 a group of American investors bought 30 square miles of undeveloped land bordering 5 miles of the east coast of the Dominican Republic in the province of La Altagracia. The land was pretty much just impenetrable jungle and bush with no access roads and only a handful of small, fishing villages dotted along the coast. But the beaches were some of the most beautiful on the island with their white sand, coconut palms, crystal clear waters and protective coral reefs. A few years later a Dominican entrepreneur Frank R. Rainieri joined them with his vision to create a resort community that respects the natural habitat while offering visitors a world class vacation experience. Señor Rainieri wisely decided to rename it Punta Cana.

In 1971 the first hotel was built in Punta Cana – the Punta Cana Club – which stood on the area now occupied by PUNTA CANA Resort & Club and in 1978 the French resort chain Club Med built a 350 room Club Med Punta Cana just north of Punta Cana Club. Sources reveal that attendants at the Punta Cana Club inauguration were laughing at Mr Rainieri and thought he was crazy to buy that land. It didn't take so long to prove he was not wrong.

But the area was still pretty isolated. The nearest town, Higuey, took 6 hours to reach. A new road was needed. The ColgatePalmolive Company, which was required to repatriate its local entities' export earnings, became involved and the new highway was built making it possible to reach Higuey in 30 minutes thus connecting Punta Cana to the rest of the island's road network.

Development

In 1982, after 8 long years of negotiation with the Dominican government, Groupo

PUNTACANA' s primitive airstrip was permitted to be developed to accommodate full sized commercial aircraft. In a joint venture with Club Med construction began and in 1984 Punta Cana International Airport (PUJ) was inaugurated with the first international flight (a twin turbo propeller aircraft) arriving from San Juan Puerto Rico. It was the world's first privately owned international airport. Without it Punta Cana would not be what it is today. In that inaugural year the airport received 2,976 passengers, in 2009 it received just under 4 million.

By providing the infrastructure Groupo PUNTACANA have turned this once inhospitable jungle coastline into a booming industry responsible for a quarter of the country's gross domestic product. Their sense of corporate responsibility is admirable – profits from the airport have been invested in community projects. Interest free educational loans, medical facilities, revolving loan funding for their worker's housing and an ecological foundation to protect and preserve the land and marine life are all part of their mission to promote sustainable development.

Today

In the meantime Punta Cana is continuing to grow with construction starting on the new Coral highway linking Punta Cana to La Romana airport bringing the journey time down from 90 mins to under 45. Punta Cana is today the largest and fastest growing tourist destination in the Caribbean and it is a popular holiday destination for people from all over the world. Punta Cana boasts more that 100 hotels & resorts and

30,000 hotel rooms spread across 40 kilometers of beautiful white sand beaches. In 2013 has been voted as best destination in the Caribbean by. Its future looks even brighter...

[Tourists who come to the area maybe unaware that Punta Cana is specifically the name of the area to the south of the airport where the very first hotel was built. Most of today's resorts are actually in Cabeza de Toro, Bavaro, Cortecito, Arena Gorda, Macao and Uvero Alto. But nearly all the hotels use the name Punta Cana in their branding even when they are not geographically located in Punta Cana. Here follows Punta Cana's history in a nutshell.

Back in 1969 a group of American investors bought 30 square miles of undeveloped land bordering 5 miles of the east coast of the

Dominican Republic in the province of La Altagracia. The land was pretty much just impenetrable jungle and bush with no access roads and only a handful of small, fishing villages dotted along the coast. But the beaches were some of the most beautiful on the island with their white sand, coconut palms, crystal clear waters and protective coral reefs.

A few years later a Dominican entrepreneur Frank R. Rainieri joined them with his vision to create a resort community that respects the natural habitat while offering visitors a world class vacation experience. At the time the area was called Punta Borrachn (Drunken Point). Se or Rainieri wisely decided to rename it Punta Cana. Together with Theodore W. Kheel, an influential American lawyer and labour arbitrator, Dominican fashion designer Oscar de la Renta and international music artist Julio Iglesias they formed the Tourist Development, Residential and Industrial Company currently known as Groupo PUNTACANA.

In 1971 the first hotel was built in Punta Cana – the Punta Cana Club which stood on the area now occupied by PUNTACANA Resort & Club. The old hotel could accommodate 40 guests and consisted of 10 rustic cabins, a clubhouse, a small employees residential area, a power plant and a short, dirt airstrip for light aircraft. In 1978 the French resort chain Club Med built a 350 room Club Med Punta Cana just north of Punta Cana Club.

But the area was still pretty isolated. The nearest town, Higuey, took 6 hours to reach. A new road was needed. The ColgatePalmolive Company, which was required to repatriate its local entities export earnings, became involved and the new highway was built making it possible to reach Higuey in 30 minutes thus connecting Punta Cana to the rest of the island's road network.

In 1982, after 8 long years of negotiation with the Dominican government, Groupo PUNTACANA's primitive airstrip was permitted to be developed to accommodate full sized commercial aircraft. In a joint venture with Club Med construction began and in 1984 Punta Cana International Airport (PUJ) was inaugurated with the first international flight (a twin turbo propeller aircraft) arriving from San Juan Puerto Rico. It was the world's first privately owned international airport. Without it Punta Cana wouldn't be what it is today. In that inaugural year the airport received 2,976 passengers, in 2009 it received just under 4 million.

Currently there are over 60 resorts in Punta Cana. These resorts, along with other tourism related business, providd employment for the ever growing local population.

To counteract Punta Cana's lack of public facilities provided by the Dominican government, Groupo PUNTACANA took upon itself the responsibility of creating and maintaining the area's public infrastructure. Access roads, security, waterworks and treatment plants, electricity, waste disposal, recycling, workers housing and schools were all established. Until recently Punta Cana was the only place on the island without daily electricity blackouts.

By providing the infrastructure Groupo PUNTACANA have turned this once inhospitable jungle coastline into a booming industry responsible for a quarter of the country's gross domestic product. Their sense of corporate responsibility is admirable – profits from the airport have been invested in community projects. Interest free educational loans, medical facilities, revolving loan funding for their worker's housing and an ecological foundation to protect and preserve the land and marine life are all part of their mission to promote sustainable development.

Unfortunately, not all tourism operations in the area practice such a high level of social and environmental awareness and poverty is still apparent on your bus ride from the airport to your 5 star resort. But Punta Cana has come a long way from it's humble origins and sustainable development is a constant, ongoing project. Idealistically one day in the future its effects will reach every part of the community.

In the meantime Punta Cana continues to grow with construction starting on the new Coral highway linking Punta Cana to La Romana airport bringing the journey time down from 90 mins to under 45. The future for Punta Cana looks bright, with it being set to remain one of the top vacation destinations in the Caribbean.]

Culture

Punta Cana is the major resort and tourist area of the Dominican Republic, and a top Caribbean vacation destination. As such, the culture is generally relaxed and almost entirely geared toward tourists. If you want to immerse yourself in the true culture of the Dominican Republic, Punta Cana would probably not be your first choice. However, if you want a fun vacation destination with white sandy beaches and luxurious allinclusive resorts (there are about 4050 AI resorts along a 25mile stretch of beach) and a Caribbean atmosphere, Punta Cana is a great choice. It's said to be slightly cheaper than many other Caribbean destinations as well. Punta Cana is relatively secluded, with nothing one could really call a "town," but the beaches are known for their beauty, and it is the feeling of being isolated from the world that keeps so many tourists coming back to Punta Cana. Punta Cana has a bit more of a European feel (topless beaches, for example) to it than other parts of the Caribbean, and many staff members at the hotels might speak broken English (Spanish is the primary language), although it has been becoming somewhat more "Globalized" in recent years.

Travel Guide

Sightseeing in Punta Cana what to see.
Complete travel guide

In the Province of La Altagracia, which is a part of the Dominican Republic, tourists can visit a beautiful island resort – Punta Cana. When looking at local views, it feels like the picture is too good to be true. Punta Cana is a paradiselike place that looks like the land of dreams. The resort has a long coastline with numerous hotels built along it. The town is very popular with foreign tourists. The nearby national parks, evergreen mangrove forests, numerous species of reptiles and tropical birds, and the diverse underwater world that is like a magnet for everyone interested in the sea depths – all these make the magnificent resort even more attractive and unforgettable.

The history of the resort started in 1969. Before that time, the territory of La Altagracia Province was mostly covered with impenetrable jungles without any roads and even paths. There were only several houses of local fishermen comfortably nestled along the coast. When American investors saw this area, they were deeply impressed by white sands and clean water. The investors decided to buy this land. Several years later, Frank Ranieri joined them. He had his own plans regarding the infrastructure of the acquired territory. He offered to build a worldclass resort in the area and call it Punta Cana.

In 1971, the first hotel building appeared on the coast of the Caribbean Sea. This hotel had only ten simple rooms and could accommodate up to forty people. One more hotel opened here eight years later, but this time the hotel had almost eight times more rooms. Despite the slowly appearing tourist infrastructure, it was very hard to reach Punta Cana because the nearest settlement was roughly six hours away. When the road to Punta Cana was finally finished, it became significantly faster to reach the resort. The first airstrip appeared here in 1982. Bavaro is the main tourist beach in Punta Cana. This beach is free to enter, and so it is usually quite crowded. Naturally, the coastal area can be bustling, especially on weekends and during the tourist season. Bavaro Beach got its name after a small settlement that is located nearby. This beach has an attraction point – a long coral reef that prevents cold water currents from mixing with the coastal water. Moreover, this naturally formed barrier protects the beach from high waves and dangerous sea creatures. These are very important factors for families, so tourists with small children enjoy visiting this beach.

Bavaro Beach is a sand area that is comfortable for swimming and sunbathing. The coastal water is shallow near the beach, and the depth increases slowly, so this beach is great for families. You can relax with your loved ones and do not worry about your child. Tall palm trees on the beach provide the necessary shadow – it is very pleasant to hide behind them in the midst of a hot day. Despite the high temperature that is typical for the resort, the sand on Bavaro Beach is always cool because it has a coral origin.

The threekilometerlong Bavaro has beach gear rental offices with equipment for different water sports and entertainment. As the coastal water is transparent and clear, many tourists want to try snorkeling and scuba diving.

Would you like to see real dolphins? During your vacation in Punta Cana, tourists are welcome to take a mesmerizing ride to the island of these cute animals. Dolphin Island Park is a floating platform that is installed at a distance from the resort area. Visitors can reach the platform on a special excursion motorboat that regularly takes passengers to the most interesting and spectacular sights of Punta Cana. The territory of the island is conventionally divided into five swimming pools, each of which is home to dolphins. Visitors can swim with these cute aquatic mammals. The swimming sessions are twentyfive minutes long.

This island differs from ordinary dolphinariums. Dolphins here are trained to be friendly and allow people to pet them. The most courageous visitors can even try to perform easy tricks with the animals. Besides cute dolphins, visitors can play with sea lions and seals. Are you short on the adrenaline in your blood? In this case, consider swimming with sharks and stingrays. After a pleasant pastime together with aquatic animals, it is incredibly pleasant to lie in a hammock sipping a cold beverage. When heading to Dolphin Island Park, tourists should keep in mind that taking photographs is allowed only for an extra fee.

To get to Punta Cana, tourists from many countries of the world need to take a connecting flight with a stop in a large European city, for example, London or Berlin. The total journey time is roughly 24 hours. For travelers from Eastern Europe, a connecting flight with a stop in Paris is the most comfortable option. The flight length is approximately fifteen hours in this case. To get to the hotel or accommodation in Punta Cana from the airport, tourists can always call a taxi or get on a local bus.

Climate, Weather and when to Go

Of course, everyone who goes to another country for new impressions and positive emotions will always be interested in the weather, choosing a time for travel, and opportunity to stay in a nice hotel. These two important things are provided there. It has a huge number of hotels that you can choose to your taste and wealth. But if compare the prices of another countries for stay at the hotel, Punta Cana opportunities will surprise you very much.

After all, service and comfort, offering at a low price at 5 and 4 star hotels of Punta Cana delight tourists. And this is one of the reasons to spend your vacation in this amazing place. On site of the most accommodations there are tennis courts and golf lessons, you can ride a horse, as well as attend a variety of restaurants, bars and clubs. You'll never be bored and lonely. Most hotels have their own beaches, and you do not have to go somewhere to enjoy the blue clear waters, dazzling white sand and charmingly radiant sun.

Hot tropical climate of Punta Cana is easily tolerated because from the sea is constantly blowing a refreshing breeze. The average annual temperature varies from 28°C to 32°C, and in peak season, which accounts for the period from April to November, the thermometer can rise up to 38°C. Punta Cana is remarkable because it does not need to wait any particular time of year to visit it, in any month the bright sun and warm Caribbean waters are waiting for you.

Weather forecasts might scare you with a rainy season. In fact, it is not so bad! It lasts from May to June and then AugustSeptember. As a rule, it looks like a few short torrential rains coming in the evening and night. So at this time of the year you can still swim and sunbathe during the day. Also, short showers may be in November and December, so watch carefully for weather forecasts. In the cold season from November to March, the usual temperature is around 20°C. In general, the weather is not capricious.

We offer 1402 hotels in Punta Cana Dominican Republic with low rates and discounts. Our reservation system provides cheap and luxury hotels in Punta Cana, hostels, motels, B&B and other budget accommodation in Punta Cana. We have excellent hotel deals in central Punta Cana. You can also book Punta Cana airport hotels at low prices. Our system is secure and absolutely chargefree.

Health and Safety

Tourists should be aware that there is a risk of contracting sicknesses from unsanitary food and water. But if you eat smart and drink smart you should be fine. Bottled water is found everywhere and the resorts provide it regularly. Always use bottled water and watch the salads that you eat, as they may be wilted from being in the hot sun too long. Cooked food should always be safe, but must be well cooked. Be careful not to get water in your mouth when you shower, and make sure to brush your teeth and rinse your toothbrush with bottled water. Be sure to keep track of your consumption of Pineapple and Coconut drinks as they can become natural laxatives to your system. Excess sun and alchohol can lead to illness. Bring your Sunscreen and use it often. Also at some of the hotels, it may smell like sewage near gardens or soil. It is NOT sewage, but it is the smell that come from the heat that contacts with the soil.

Be advised that only Potable water is used for making Ice, so no worries about ice.

There is also a slight risk of contracting malaria from mosquitoes, malaria is endemic in the rural areas of the Dominican Republic that border Haiti. Although all resorts spray regularly for mosquitos be sure to bring an insect repellent with 25% "deet" for avoiding mosquito bites.

Here is a quick important tips

Drink lots of (bottled) water! Have a glass of water for every drink or at least every two alcoholic beverages.

Some people take Pepto Bismol in the morning or before every meal as a preventative measure. There are side effects to beware of (weird black tongue among them!) as with all medication so though you are using it for one battle, make sure that you know what you are ingesting. It can also act to stop you up so you won't get diahrrea but it could lead to the opposite problem. The nature of the product is that it provides protection by coating your stomach. You should beware of that if you are taking some other medication orally which you are expecting will be absorbed through the stomach walls. Effectiveness will be blocked.

If you get sick anyway and start taking Immodium, stop the Pepto Bismol therapy immediately. They don't mix. If you are staying around the hotel and can find the diahrrea merely an inconvenience, wait it out and flush your system as opposed to stopping nature from doing its job. See if you can only take the Immodium if you are heading out on an excursion or flying home. If you have something in your system that needs to be eliminated, beware that taking Immodium or something like that that is keeping it in your body could make you suffer with cramps and other abdominal pain or discomfort. It really is best in that situation to lay low, stay out of the sun, eat bananas and bread and white rice, drink lots of water, and let it pass in the natural way.

Some people bring a prescription for the antibiotic Cipro with them. As far as antibiotics go, it's a strong one and you should be sure that you follow the instructions provided for diagnosing the correct time to start taking it. Generally, it's when you see the presence of blood and once you've had the diahrrea for a full 24 hours. It's not recommended for those under the age of 16 years and it's not to be taken when you have a stomach ache or general diahrrea. Many Travelers follow a natural course of prevention by means of acidophilus and probiotic dairy products. Both act to increase the good bacteria in your system to counteract nasty bacteria. You can start that treatment before you leave home and continue it for the duration of your vacation. Coconut is a laxative and bananas are a natural binder. Bear both in mind!

The hotels will use only potable water in the restaurants and for making ice, as well as the making of coffee and washing of vegetables. Make sure you don't have accidents brushing with tap water or consuming shower water. As a rule, avoid all rare or raw protein products, like eggs and shellfish, and if any fish or meat looks suspicious, avoid it since there will surely be something else for you to select. Always go prepared and watch what you eat and watch for symptoms and make sure that you have travel medical insurance. If you have any known plant allergies or interactions, don't try mamajuana (an indigenous drink of the Dominican Republic consisting of a generally unknown combo of bark and twigs [each batch is going to be a bit different so that's why you may not know what's in one compared to another] soaked in rum and red wine and honey). Other than its potency and the fun factor of drinking a lot of it, some people find that they experience an adverse reaction to something in it.

There are lime leaves in the woods that are poison to the skin too so keep your arms and legs in the vehicle if going through the woods on an Outback trip. Just show caution and be smart in all that you do. Know the benefits and reasons why you'd take any medication that you take with you, as well as when it should be administered and when it should be stopped, and get to know the expected side effects. If you have the medical insurance and anything happens that has you worried, go to the resort doctor to set your mind at ease or start treatment. The opinion of a professional who knows about most of what tourists will meet with can be very consoling. They are well used to the symptoms and treatment of various stomach ailments too: the difference between Caribbean food poisoning, the stomach flu and a hangover.

Electricity

One of the most common questions asked is "Will our electric devices <you fill in the device> work in the DR?" or "Will we need a converter?". The quick answer is "Maybe", refer to this as Electricity 101 or the three bears description.

To start off, the electricity in the DR is the same as in North America. It's alternating current with a nominal voltage of 115/120 volts and the frequency is 60 hertz (cycles per second). You guys from across the pond have a nominal voltage of 220/240 and a frequency of 50 hertz. This brings in a whole other set of issues, so this article will cover that separately. Normally, the frequency is not a big issue for most devices; it's the voltage and physical connections.

For North Americans (and other places that use this system)

So, you might ask, if the electricity is the same, then why can't we just plug in our device and go?

Well, yes, it's the same, but the physical connection to it is slightly different; just enough to cause problems. If you examine a conventional North American electrical socket, you will notice that there are three holes. Two look like small slots and the third looks like a "U". If you look even closer, you will notice that one of the slots is slightly larger. Each hole serves a different function and the shape/size identifies that function (hot, neutral and safety ground). Now, if you look at the cord that plugs into this socket, you will see one of two types. It will either have three prongs on it, to line up with the socket, or it may have only two flat blades. One of those blades will have little ears on it, making it larger than the other one. There is a reason for all this, and it's called safety. The system is designed so that the plug can only be inserted one way. It's called polarization. This is where the difficulty starts, since they don't use this system in the DR. Their plugs will go in either way.

First, the socket in the DR will have only two holes. Usually it will accept either two flat blades or a European type round pin. Obviously, anything with a three prong plug isn't going to fit. Unfortunately, the North American two prong plug usually won't fit either, because in their infinite wisdom, they designed it so that the two slots are the same size, and yes, it's the small one. You may luck out, and countless tourists ahead of you may have jammed the plug in and enlarged (read as 'broken') the socket so that the cord will fit.

Oh, and there's another complication. Sometimes you will find a socket that is recessed about a centimeter (1/2" for those of you who aren't metric). This causes issues for those little transformer plugs that they use on the battery chargers for cameras, cell phones and the like. Because of the recess, the prongs on the transformer box won't physically reach the socket.

This is what you will likely see at some resorts:

Health

Occasionally, you will see a forum post warning about Malaria. Malaria is endemic to Hispanola, especially the western side (Haiti) and is transmitted by mosquitoes. Please do not rely on advice from anyone on these forums as to what to do concerning your, or your childrens health. Please note. The World Health Organisation advises government bodies on risks and on Malaria policy, however, the UK National Health

Service advises the travelling UK public on health matters through web sites listed below. You are therefore advised to take note of the contents of these links and consult your Doctor or Practice Nurse for advice on all vaccinations including the use of malaria prophylaxis before travelling to this area.

Note. <u>The majority of travel insurance companies have disclaimers in their Travel insurance policy wording booklet:</u>

Typically. We will not cover the following: Any costs that are a result of a tropical disease, if you have not had the recommended vaccinations or taken the recommended medication.

<u>Food and Drink</u>

The best way to ensure a great vacation is not to overindulge with food and drink. All food served at the resorts is safe to eat, even lettuce, raw fruit, and salads. Please eat and drink in moderation and you should suffer no ill effects.

The hotels use only purified water for cooking and for making ice. If they do not they will tell you otherwise. Most have strict quality control procedures in place regarding food and drink and the cleanliness of their premises. If you are unsure about anything you should ask when being served.

If you travel outside the resort, drink only bottled water, and drinks with no ice in them. If you are not sure of something do not eat or drink it. Do not take chances.

Resorts can have several bars. Normally they are found in the lobby, at the beach and by the pool. Just ask for a drink and you will be served. If you do not want alcohol in your drink just say "sin (no) alcohol". The local beer is Presidente. The local liquor is called Normandy or Columbus. Some 5 star resorts do have International brands of liquor available. Tropical drinks and cocktails are also available, e.g. nana Mama, Strawberry Daquiri, and Pina Colada. Please note, that many tropical drinks contain coconut milk, which is a natural laxative!

If you become sick and wish to self medicate, Immodium, AlkaSeltzer/PeptoBismal/Tums, and Tylenol can be used to alleviate the symptoms, but you should follow the advice of the enclosed leaflets/printed on the box and never exceed the recommended dose. You are advised to take them with you, because they can be expensive to purchase locally! If you have a stomach upset and are unsure of your symptoms it is best to consult the resort local doctor.

Things to Do

Overview of the Area

Punta Cana consists of nearly 50 allinclusive resorts along a near 30 mile stretch of the most beautiful soft white sandy beaches, lots of swaying palm trees, a near constant gentle breeze, and some of the most vivid turqoise blue waters you'll ever see anywhere.

However, don't believe what some of the resort people tell you regarding safety. Since 2006 Punta Cana has been reported as having one of the lowest crime rates in the world, mostly because of the low drug crime here. Statements, primarily from resorts who are protecting their market share, saying this area is NOT safe, do not benefit the Punta Cana area or the people who live here (hopefully the resort directors are reading this as you are also hurting yourselves too). It could be they are saying this so they are not liable for stupid people who get crazy on vacation outside the resort, and show disrespect to the locals.   But also because of the new competition of so many gorgeous vacation condos for rent that are on or near the beach, and a short walk to all the modern shopping and dining amenties... which are often much more affordable than staying at an allinclusive resort.

In fact, there are many POLITUR (police just for tourist) who do nothing else but scope the area making sure tourist are safe and having fun.

Assuming the resort you are staying at is located in or near El Cortecito or Bavaro... It is quite OK to get off the resort and check out the local area and mingle with the locals and expats. In fact, new sidewalks are now under construction connecting the Bavaro and El Cortecito Los Corales areas together, and should be completed by late April, 2012. There is a whole amazing world outside the entrance of your resort. Punta Cana is quite safe and the local people are very friendly and helpful. Of course, no matter where you travel in the world, you can't get "stupid". Also remember, the locals will approach you in regard to selling their souvineers. Keep in mind, they also have families to feed, and will try to sell you stuff for more than you should pay . But if you're happy with your negotiated price, and they're happy... then everyone is happy. If you don't want to be bothered, kindly say "Not today thank you"... or, if you want to impress them with Spanish just say "No hoy Gracias" (the "h" in hoy is silent).

If you're not staying at a resort further from the El Cortecito or Bavaro... and want to get off the resort, just take a taxi the drive to these areas, (unless you are staying in Uvero Alto) is within a 1020 minute drive away.

There are now many people from all over the world that live, work or have retired to Punta Cana/ El Cortecito/ Bavaro; hence, English is now heard almost everywhere. These people, called "expats" are mostly from Canada,Spain, France, Italy, United States, Germany, and recently from various places in South America and Russia. In addition to the many Dominicans (and Haitians the true worker bees here), it's truely amazing to see how many people from all over the world live and work harmoniously together here in Punta Cana.

Getting around can be challenging because there are only a few directional signs and actual street signs and nobody really uses them. Several streets weave around different communities and resorts, and many do not follow the beach... so its important to know in advance how to manuver around so you can find all the cool places like: Beach bars, restaurants (on and off the beach), excursion companies, Casino's, Discos (a couple of them are in caves), golf courses, big grocery stores, new and modern shopping malls, bakeries, ATM machines, IMAX Cinema movie theatres (where you can buy popcorn and a beer), Hard Rock Cafe Punta Cana, a huge and very nice mall, cash exchange places, tons of other beautiful beaches, ship wrecks, adventure tours (2tracks)... and other places off the tourist strip where prices are better... the list is endless. Its highly recommended you check out either Saona Island or Catalina Island (full day tours).

Oh, and the name "Punta Cana" is used loosely. Besides the International Airport, there are actually only a few things to do in Punta Cana. In fact, most of the people that live in Punta Cana come to Bavaro or El Cortecito for the beaches and night life.

Dominican Cigars

Dominican cigars are also some of the finest rolled anywhere. You will find a lot of vendors that sell cigars in their stores, on the beach or on the streets.

Beware: Cuban and Dominican counterfeits are big business!

Be very careful as there are a lot of fakes out there; many are secondquality made from scraps and sweepings.

The best come from the area around the growing fields in Villa Gonzales to the historical town of Tamboril outside of Santiago.

Do a google search for Dominican cigars and you will see many places where you can order online and what the real prices are for these. Then, when someone on the beach asks you for $50 for a box of you will know they are fakes. A decent cigar will cost at least $4 usd up to $15.00 for a truly superb smoke.

Stay away from the duty free cigars, they are expensive their genuinity can be suspect.

Remember: a good cigar is not cheap.

Recommended places to purchase authentic cigars in Punta Cana Bavaro...

Bavaro/Punta Cana

Don Lucas...the area's largest producer of cigars and selection of world renowned cigars...complimentary pick up from your resort

La Reina Dominicana, in La Plaza de Brisas/Bavaro, handrolled ClassA Cigars and handmade Amber and Larimar Jewlery store. All

Cigars handrolled right there, FREE Roundtrip Transfers from all

Nicole Boutique, located in the White Sands Golf Course Club House offers handrolled cigars. You will also find original jewelry, made with Larimar (Dominican national stone), amber, fresh waterpearl and other semiprecious stones. They offer free roundtrip transportation from all hotels

La Romana (40 minute drive) Free pickups from Bayahibe and Dominicus Monday, Thursday 10AM

Tabacalera de Garcia, Casa de Campo La Romana, Dominican Republic

One of the largest handmade cigar factories in the world, employing more than 4,000 people.

Here you will see the proud handwork of the cigar industry's most experienced craftsmen and women. Their Cigar Shop carries a wide selection of premium Dominican cigars.

Monday Friday: 8 am 5 pm | Saturday: 8 am 12 pm (Tours by appointment only)

La Flor Dominicana Cigar Factory Experience La Romana, Dominican Republic

Hailed by Cigar Aficionado as "the most creative manufacturer in the cigar business", La Flor Dominicana Cigar Factory consistently produces some of the hottest brands on the market today. Come visit the most amazing boutique handmade cigar factory in the world, all under the watchful eyes of cigar legend Master Blender Jose Seijas.

Daily: 8 am 6:30pm (Tours open to public)

Vivaldi Cigars, Cabeza de Toro Punta Cana/Bavaro, Dominican Republic

Vivaldi Cigar Lounge is the most recent addition to the prestigious Vivaldi Cigar brand. It is open for visitors from the Punta Cana/Bavaro area. Situated on the beach of Cabeza de Toro, Punta Cana, visitors can enjoy a complimentary smoking seminar on the beach with the finest hand rolled Dominican cigars. Free transportation is provided to and from your hotel. Seminars are given in English, Dutch, German, Spanish and French.

Golf in Punta Cana

Punta Cana in the Dominican Republic is a widely known world class golf destination offering many varied courses. Among them three oceanside golf courses, Punta Espada at Cap Cana , Corales Golf Club and the 27 holes of La Cana Golf Club. If you're a serious golfer you look "Bucket List Courses" and for names like Tom Fazio, PB Dye and Jack Nicklaus you should try Punta Cana.

Barcelo' Bavaro The Lakes Golf Course

Iberostate Bavaro Golf & Club

Cana Bay Palace – Hard Rock Golf Club

White Sands Golf Club

Punta Blanca Golf Course

Roco Ki Golf Club – The Faldo Legacy Course

Catalonia Caribe Golf Club

Residencial Cayena Golf Club

With dozens of worldclass designer golf courses surrounded by magnificent unspoiled nature, breathtaking coastlines and lush green fairways, the Dominican Republic is the new "in" destination for golf. Nine of the country's golf courses are included in Golfweek Magazine's 2010 list of the top 50 courses in the Caribbean and Latin America. Former U.S. presidents Bill Clinton and George H.W. Bush, plus sports champions and golf enthusiasts from around the world come to enjoy 28 golf courses designed by golf legends such as Pete Dye, P.B. Dye, Jack Nicklaus, Robert Trent Jones Sr., Gary Player, Tom Fazio, Nick Faldo, Nick Price and Greg Norman.

Visitors to the Dominican Republic don't have to worry about bringing golf clubs or their level of experience. Each course offers golf clubs for rent at reasonable prices and golf lessons from recognized professionals. Whatever your handicap is, the golf courses of the Dominican

Republic promise you a unique and challenging experience.

Nightlife

Nightlife In Punta Cana

Mangu: Located in the Grand Occidental Flamenco Resort , this is the world famous disco with two floors of amazing music to satisfy all your fantasies. Mangu is a dream world that is quite unforgettable. The first floor will get you moving with beautiful Merengue, Bachata, Reggaeton and HipHop music. A lot of Latin and Caribbean influence on this level. Sometimes the famous "Rollerblader" may come downstairs on the stage or do some breakdancing on the dance floor. This level of the disco is awesome! You will never stop dancing unless you need to quench your thirst with another drink ,from the sexy bar tenders. As you start to walk up the

"Stairway to Heaven" you will hear some sexy House beats spinning. They also play some Trance, many other styles of House and some Techno beats. This place is a dream world with a VIP lounge with low white leather couches , a raised DJ Booth, and the bar area lit with purple neon lights, They have white cloth tied together like a swing for when the shows are put on by the dancers. This disco is truly one to meet a million of your fantasies im one night! The dancers are so fun and love to put on a show for everyone. Once you get on the dance floor it is hard to leave beacuse it is such a fun place. Dance from dusk till dawn! There are many other surprises this disco brings to the people, so if you go to Dominican Republic in the Bavaro area, you must go to Disco Mangu. It would be a shame if you passed this amazing opportunity by!

Ladies if you go there single you can expect to get attention from the many Dominican men who attend the disco. This bar attracts many locals and tourists. It is the # 1 disco in Punta Cana! It opens at 11 pm and doesn't close until people start clearing out.

Disco Pacha: Located in the Riu Resorts, this disco club is one of the first to become a big attraction for the ones who love the nightlife. With concerts of local famous bands and an eccentric combination of International and Caribbean rhythms, it is a guarantee for you to experience the night of your life. Request your favorite cocktail and let yourself be driven by the rhythms.

<u>Areito:</u> Located in Caribe Club Princess this is one of the newest discos to the Punta Cana Area. Decorated with Indigenes elements and Aborigine cultural objects and just by the name you will see why this disco is a favorite "The dance of the Gods". In that spirit you can enjoy the most exclusive atmosphere. With live shows and events that are organized all the time one knows that you will have a fulfilled night.

<u>Una Mas:</u> Located across from the princess tower casino this is the Newest lounge in Punta Cana. With the style of new york and glam of europe it is sure to be the next hot spot in the DR. With a special VIP area like no other, and music that is constantly updated, you will be sure to be impressed. Very close to some of the other clubs so easy access from almost anywhere you are. Try there house special shot called NO MAS

you'll understand the meaning after you take one!

Punta Cana Bar Crawl: the first bar crawl run in Punta Cana. Tourists will be taken to 45 among the best bars/clubs in the area enjoying free shots, drink discounts, free entries and more.

Off the Beaten Path

Punta Cana Bavaro has developed over the past decade into the leading destination in the Caribbean. Gone are the days when you could hardly leave the resort due to poor roads and directions. Most main roads in the region now sport fresh hardtop, although signage can be a bit confusing at times.

You have many options for seeing what makes the region what it is...and what it was! Organized tours, both based on mass travel and small group travel are available and highly recommended for those visiting for the first time. Independent travel is best left to those vacationers with a few trips here under their belts. A good representation of car rental facilities now exist, but again....UNLESS you understand Dominican driving...best try another option.

The region now has local bus service that circles the area. Just stand on the side of the road and see what happens. Guaguas are usually older Toyota 30 seater buses and are a very cheap way to get from point A to B. You can tell the driver where you want to go and he will drop you off accordingly.

The new Autopista (expressway) between Punta Cana and La Romana means that a day trip to La

Romana and Bayahibe are now within easy reach!

Reserva Ecologica Ojos Indigenas

The Indigenous Eyes Ecological Reserve is one of the only private forest reserves in Punta Cana and one of its best kept secrets. The reserve is owned and managed by the PUNTACANA Ecological Foundation and forms part of 1,500 acres of the Puntacana Resort & Club property set aside as conservation land. You can take a refreshing dip in on one of the twelve lagoons the Taino Indians called "eyes." Many believe they hold medicinal properties. This is really one of the most unique and unexplored jewels of Punta Cana.

To explore the reserve without a guide, you must be a guest at PUNTACANA Resort & Club

(.puntacana.com). For guests of hotels other than Puntacana Resort & Club, you can participate in a guided 2hour tour with experiened guides. Guests will be provided transportation to and from their hotel. Bring your bathing suit as you will have an opportunity to swim in at least one of the freshwater lagoons. The Ecological Foundation also offers a number of unique excursions including segway tours, horseback riding, and adventure cars.

To learn more, please contact 18294701367 or 18294701121 or write to info@segwayecotour.com

History of the Indigenous Eyes

Indigenous Eyes is one of the only private forest reserves in Punta Cana. The reserve forms a part of 1,500 acres of the property set aside as conservation land. The reserve is owned and managed by the PUNTACANA Ecological Foundation. The Foundation and a prestigious group of national and international collaborators conduct research, investigation, and environmental education programs in the reserve through the Center for Sustainability. The reserve has twelve fresh water lagoons. An underground freshwater river known locally as Yauya feeds the lagoons and eventually makes its way to the ocean.

If you walk to the beach directly in front of the reserve entrance and look closely amongst the remaining mangrove trees you can see Yauya emptying into the ocean. The ground in Punta Cana is primarily limestone coral made of fossilized oceanic material that has been pushed above sea level over thousands of years. If you look closely you can find fossilized seashells, sponges and other marine relics in the rocks throughout the reserve. The annual rainfall in Punta Cana can reach 1,300 mm, but the porous nature of the limestone causes the water to filter through quickly to the groundwater. For this reason there are few rivers in Punta Cana. Renowned historian and Dominican scholar Bernardo Vega has given each of the twelve lagoons a unique name from the native Taino language.

The reserve is categorized as a "Transition Zone SubTropical Forest," since flora and fauna characteristic of both the Dry and Humid SubTropical Forests can be found. Reptiles from the Anolis genus are abundant in this area, as well as small green snakes, frogs and other lizards. But not to worry, there are no venomous snakes on the Island of Hispaniola. The reserve has over 500 plant species, 36% of which live nowhere else in the world but the Dominican Republic. Red Land Crabs are common in the Ecological Reserve. Once a year, these crabs climb up from their protective crevices by the thousands to mate. Over 100 different species of birds have been identified in Punta Cana during the winter migration season. Wasps, butterflies, ants and termites are common in Indigenous Eyes. As you are walking, you will see large brown nests in the trees. These are signs that the forest is healthy because the termites that live in the nests break down the dead and dying materials and transform it into fertile habitat.

The reserve is guided by a Leave No Trace policy, visitors are asked to help maintain the natural beauty of Indigenous Eyes by disposing of trash in designated containers and being respectful of the plant and animal life that you encounter. Visitors are also asked to swim only in lagoons that are accessible for swimming and be careful as you enter and exit the lagoons. The reserve is open daily from sunup to sundown.

The PUNTACANA Ecological Foundation manages the Indigenous Eyes Reserve as part of its ongoing efforts to protect and restore the natural resources of Punta Cana and contribute to the sustainable development of the Dominican Republic.

Segway EcoTour

A worthwhile , fun tour of Playa Blanca and Punta Cana Resort and golf club. The Segways are very easy to ride , they are auto balanced so you don't have to worry about falling off , helmets are provided. You have a guide to lead the group and makes sure everyone is doing ok . If you cannot manage the Segway a golf cart is available.

You tour Playa Blanca .. a beautiful , white, sandy beach with crystal clear sea. A 10 minute stop at the beach is a welcome break to have a dip and cool off. Then you are on your way again , throgh Punta Cana Resort and a stop at the nature reserve by the lagoon. On returning to base you are given a welcome coconut drink and the chance to buy souviner photographs .. a nice reminder of a wonderful day .

Shopping

The shopping in Punta Cana is not exactly what brings the tourists in, but it is still something that you can add to your list of things to do in Punta

Cana. Fortunately finding shops in Punta Cana is easier than ever. Punta Cana has a variety of fantastic places to go shopping. No matter what you're looking for, whether it's Americanstyle shopping malls or authentic Dominican markets, you're sure to find it while shopping in Punta Cana.

Unless you are booking a stay at one of the vacation rentals in Punta Cana, you will likely be staying at one of the all inclusive resorts. Most of these resorts offer shops of their own. The stores at the resorts typically sell souvenirs, clothing items, beachrelated goods, and jewelry. It's also common to be able to buy handicrafts and other locally made products at some of the resorts, including cigars and rum.

Punta Cana has many shopping plazas, stocked with Dominican & Caribbean crafts and unique gift ideas: silver and hand made souvenirs, handrolled cigars, rum and ceramics. Shopping plazas in Punta Cana are in the open air and consist of many small shops:

Plaza Bavaro

Located next to the entrance to Occidental Flamenco Hotel is one of the largest shopping center filled with Dominican souvenirs and stores that offer all the extras that you might need on your trip, anything from Drug stores to beach clothing. Shopping at Plaza Bavaro provides a great opportunity to mingle with the locals while on vacation in Punta Cana. The Plaza is open every day from 9:00 am to 7:00 pm and includes many gifts shops, a calling center,

Internet center, banks, restaurants, pharmacy, jewellery store and various boutiques.

Plaza Bávaro can be a great place to go, but only if you're willing to haggle. Many of the prices at this shopping plaza are overinflated, and if you purchase what's on the price tag, you're probably overpaying. The nice thing about this plaza is that there are a lot of locals that shop here, so you can get a sense of where everyday Dominicans do their shopping. The downside is that many visitors to Punta Cana feel that the vendors and store owners at Plaza Bávaro can be too pushy in trying to convince you to buy something, but if you're prepared for that, and you're ready to haggle, it can be a great place to go shopping in Punta Cana.

Beach Shopping Plazas

Along the beach of Bavaro there are many places where you can find shopping plazas with many shops where to buy some local souvenirs:

– Plaza Bibijagua, located in proximity of the resorts IFA Villas Bavaro and Barcelo Palace Deluxe

– Jellyfish Shopping Center, located close the resort Melia Caribe Tropical

– Galerias El Pirata, located between the resorts Now Larimar and Barcelo Dominican Beach, in Los Corales

– El Cortecito, located next to the resort Presidential Suites

Downtown Mall

One of the main signs of the evolution of the Punta Cana district is the recent development of Downtown Punta Cana and the shopping center

Downtown Mall. The new shopping center has been inaugurated in December 2018, consisting of 60 stores, 3 levels, and the first surfing pool in the country, as well as a large and modern indoor parking with capacity for 300 vehicles that complements its front parking. Located at the most convenient point, where the Boulevard Turístico del Este and Avenida Barceló meet, is today a mandatory step for the communities of Verón, Bávaro, Friusa, El Cortecito and all the hotels in the area. The new shopping center supplies the services and entertainment needs of the residents of this growing tourist destination.

The project has important business partners, such as supermarket chain Jumbo, main anchor of the project, Claro, Banco Popular, Scotiabank, Banco del Progreso, Dominos Bistro, Carol Pharmacy, Gastro Gourmet, Ice Cream Bon, Café

Santo Domingo, Universal Insurance, National Car Rental among others, that have positioned it as a point of reference and, a short time after its opening, being visited by more than 200,000 people monthly.

Bluemall Punta Cana

One of the most complete commercial centers of the Caribbean. The shopping mall is located just 2 kilometers from Punta Cana International Airport, less than 35 kilometers from all Bavaro and Punta Cana hotels and only 2 hours from Santo Domingo by the Coral Highway. BlueMall Puntacana consists of an airconditioned single level, with shops of great international brands, excellent national and international restaurants, a wide offer of services and a fantastic entertainment area. With its unparalleled shopping and entertainment experience, all in one place, this shopping center is undoubtedly the perfect complement to the exceptional hotel offer of the eastern part of the country.

BlueMall Punta Cana has a magnificent outdoor amphitheater with capacity for more than three thousand people and an amazing spectacle of dancing waters, lights and sound. The splendid view of the fountain can be enjoyed from the terraces of Los Burros Geniales, Bachata Rosa by SBG and Hard Rock Cafe.

Palma Real Shopping Village (Closing soon)

(At the beginning of 2020 this Shopping Plaza is closing down to leave space for the new Theme Park Katmandu)

While Plaza Bavaro and Beach Plazas are an excellent place to rummage through a variety of goods, Palma Real Shopping Village is one of the best places to go if you're looking to do some serious shopping. You will find the Palma Real Shopping Village near the Cocotal Golf Course, the Paradisus Palma Real Resort, and the Melia Caribe Tropical. Basically, this is a good place to go shopping in Punta Cana if you're looking for something a little more upscale and a little closer to the kind of shopping experiences you can have in the U.S.

Please note that the prices at this mall are a bit inflated (most people say it's pricey). Inside the Shopping Center there are 2 banks and a large super market (Plaza Lama) which makes this place very popular among locals. After the opening of the newest BlueMall and DownTown Mall, this shopping center has lost some appeal and many brands (like Hard Rock Cafe, Outback

Steakhouse, and others) have moved to the new shopping areas DownTown Mall and BlueMall.

San Juan Shopping Center

Once the region's most complete shopping experience, located at Coco Loco intersection. San Juan Shopping Center is a shopping destination, offering a sevenscreen movie theater, many wellknown jewelry and clothing brand shops, and other shops such as a pharmacy, electronics and banks. After the opening of the new DownTown Mall just next door, this shopping center is not popular like in the past and many shops inside (specially in the second floor) are now closed or empty.

Caribbean Street

Caribbean Street is a fantastic place to go shopping in Punta Cana. With its adorable, brightly colored shops and palm trees lining the street, it has a very authentic Caribbean vibe. There are a variety of stores to choose from as well. Besides practical stores, such as a pharmacy and a gym, Caribbean Street has a number of gift shops and boutiques selling oneofakind clothing. There's also a Harrison's Jewelers, which makes some of the finest jewelry in the Caribbean. If you're up for a splurge, it's a great way to get something unique so you'll always remember your trip to Punta Cana.

Mundo Autentico & Don Lucas Cigar Factory

Located in the Don Lucas Cigars Factory, this is a complementary shop to buy some local souvenirs and Dominican products for those visiting the cigars factory. Free Transportation is included and this free tour is offered by the most of the hotels in Punta Cana.

Choco Museo

If you like chocolate this is a place to visit. Includes visit of the cacao and chocolate museum, chocolate factory, chocolate tasting, chocolate making workshop and more. Free transportation from any hotel in Punta Cana. Located in the same site of Don Lucas Cigars Factory and Mundo Autentico.

La Reina Dominicana

This combo store is particularly indicated for those looking for some good authentic jewelry and cigars (they make their own cigars there). Prices are very affordable and probably the best among the various shopping tours offered at the hotels. Free roundtrip transportation is included as well.

In addiction, you can also get some handmade jewelry and other knickknacks from the beach and street vendors, so Punta Cana shopping definitely isn't limited to the main stores and shopping centers. There's more to shopping in Punta Cana than you might have originally anticipated, so should you get the itch to shop during your visit, you can surely do so.

Tips

– Bartering with the Punta Cana beach vendors and at the impromptu local markets is encouraged and can only add excitement to your overall Punta Cana shopping experience. Bargain especially for cash purchases – don't forget to ask for a discount, which may be as high as 40% off the asking price.

– Note that in Punta Cana, many places are cash only. Even places that accept credit cards will likely give you a discount of some kind if you're willing to pay in cash.

– Speaking of cigars, the Dominican Republic produces more of them than any other country in the world, including Cuba. In case you want to take some cigars home with you, some of the bestknown brands are La Aurora, Arturo Fuente, and Montecristo.

(Be aware that most of the cigars sold on the beach or on the streets are fake so don't make the mistake to spend a lot of dollars for counterfeit cigars.)

– In addition to cigars, rum is something that many tourists look to buy when doing some Punta Cana shopping. Bermudez, Brugal, and Barcelo are the top rum brands in the Dominican Republic. Just remember that airlines put restrictions on liquid carryons, so if you are taking rum home with you, it will have to go in the suitcase.

– If you are looking specifically for jewelry when doing some Punta Cana shopping, head to Harrison's Jewelry Store near the Iberostar Resort. It's renowned for its quality, and is considered to be one of the top jewelry makers in the Caribbean.

San Juan Shopping Center: The region's most complete shopping experience, located at Coco Loco intersection. Everything from QUALITY and

UNIQUE gifts to everyday clothing and appliances! Even an Ikea Catalog store!

Plaza Bavaro/Bavaro Shopping Center: Located next to the entrance to Occidental Flamenco Hotel until Bavaro Princess hotel. A mix of modern and traditional gifts, mixed with some real estate offices and restaurants.One of the largest shopping center filled with Dominican souvenirs and stores that offer all the extras that you might need on your trip, anything from Drug stores to beach clothing.

Plaza Punta Cana: Located across from Occidental Flamenco, this shopping center offers a wide variety of the Dominican Souvenirs and to help you choose you will find an excited group of vendors.

<u>El Cortesito FleaMarket:</u> located right next to the beach you will find several stores with a wide selection of Dominican Souvenirs and Caribbean style clothing. You will also find several restaurants , the fabled Capitan Cook's and the new kid on the block...making a great first impression, Casa de Piedra.

<u>Palma Real Shopping:</u> If you long for the taste and style of home, look no further. PRS is a modern shopping area with opportunities to purchase top shelf gifts and clothing, as well as giving you the back home tastes of Tony Romas and Hard Rock Café

Dining

Why would I want to go out to restaurants in Punta Cana? This is a question we get asked all the time. The answer is simple: –sometimes resort food can get a little boring (even if it''s really good) and it''s nice to see something different. Most often we just want a break from the resort, see some different scenery and try out some new flavors. Other times, we have been off sightseeing or shopping and just happen by one and can''t resist.

In Punta Cana there is a large variety of restaurants for every taste and you can enjoy exquisite specialties while watching beautiful sceneries. Vacationers in Punta Cana can dine in formal restaurants that serve filet mignon and lobster, or they can enjoy a more laid back and casual setting while dining on the island's national dish of la bandera.

Traditional Dominican cuisine is basically a mixture of Spanish, Taino and African gastronomy and consists mainly of rural recipes elaborated with simple ingredients. Here in Punta Cana, and even within your resort, you can easily find restaurants and dishes from different countries. You might find good food, good value, and friendly service, but keep in mind that the farther you go off the beaten track, the more unlikely it is that English will be spoken.

Here below you can find a complete list with all the most important restaurants you can dine in Punta Cana arranged by type of cuisine, with address and contact number, with our special recommendations depending on the kind of experience you're looking for.

(If you know a restaurant not listed below and you want to add it, please feel free to contact us and we will change the list).

International

Acentos Bistro — Galerias Punta Cana Village
809.959.0161

Bamboo — Punta Cana Resort & Club
809.959.2262

Brot Bagel Shop — Galerias Punta Cana Village
809.959.2007

Citrus — Los Corales, Bavaro 809.455.2026
(recommended)

Club Aqua Mare — Marina Cap Cana
908.469.7342

Batu — Plaza El Dorado, Los Corales

Fuego Gastro by Martin Berasategui — Hotel
Paradisus 809.687.9923

Garry's Good Times — Los Corales

Hard Rock Cafe — Palma Real Shopping Village
809.552.0594

Huracan Cafe – Playa Bavaro 809.552.1046 / 809.754.5405

Juanillo – Juanillo Beach, Cap Cana 809.543.2881

Kukua Beach Club – Arena Gorda, Punta Blanca 829.943.8118

La Palapa – Caleton Beach Club, Cap Cana 809.469.7469

O Sole Mio – Veron Crossroad, Veron 809.455.1143

Onno's – El Cortecito 809.552.0376

Outside In – Av. Alemania, Bavaro 809.552.0167

Noah – Plaza Paseo San Juan, Av. Barcelo 809.455.1060 (recommended)

Nam Nam – Los Corales, Bavaro 809.988.3176 (recommended)

Pastrata – Av. Alemania, El Cortecito

829.645.6767 (recommended)

Playa Blanca — Punta Cana Resort & Club
809.959.2714

Privilege — The Golf Suites, Cocotal
809.677.0012

Ragazzi — Palma Real Shopping Village
809.455.7828

Soles Chill Out Beach Bar — Los Corales, Playa
Bavaro   809.910.4371

Simon Mansion — Hard Rock Hotel —
809.731.0094 (recommended)

The Moon — El Cortecito, Playa Bavaro
829.643.7039

French

Chez Mon Ami — Plaza Nautica, Bavaro
8095526714

Grill & Steak House

Outback Steakhouse – Palma Real Shopping Village 809.552.8878

Chef Pepper – San Juan Shopping Center 809.466.2333

Tony's Roma – Palma Real Shopping Center 809.552.8880

Cut's and Grill – Av. Alemania, Los Corales 809.455.2885

Mexican

Andale Guey – Av. Espana, Plaza Mayoral 809.552.1418

El Burrito – Palma Real Shopping Village 809.952.6045

Taco – Ciudad Las Canas, Cap Cana 809.469.7575

Spanish

Carlota Restaurant — Plaza San Juan 809 953 1461

El Tablao — Galerias Punta Cana Village 809.959.3008

Passion by Martin Berasategui — Paradisus Palma Real Resort   809.688.5000

Cuban

Don Pio — Plaza Turquesa, Los Corales 809 455 7373

Asian

Zen — Galerias Punta Cana Village 809.959.0387

Balicana — Los Corales, Bavaro   829.898.4479 (recommended)

Akikomo — Plaza Proa   809.552.1644

Dominican / Criolla

Carbon – Galerias Punta Cana Village 809.959.0018

La Posada de Glady's – Av. Alemania, Los Corales (recommended)

La Casita de Yeya – Cruce Coco Loco 809 466 1096

Fast Food

Burger King – Veron Crossroad 809.552.9909

Wendy's – Galerias Punta Cana Village 809.959.9717

Italian

Ama – Calle Barcelona, Bavaro

Bella Napoli – Avenida Alemania, Plaza Nautica 829 348 3538

D'Angelos – Los Corales, Bavaro 809.552.0881

Il Cappuccino — Marina Cap Cana, Cap Cana 809.469.7095

Cappuccino Mare — Av. Estados Unidos, Bavaro 809.468.4646

Huracan Cafe — Los Corales, Playa Bavaro 809.552.1046

Mamma Luisa — Galerias Punta Cana Village 809.959.2013

Papa Jonhs — Palma Real Shopping Center 809.552.8800

Pizza Hut — San Juan City Center 809.466.2008

Venezia — Av. Alemania, Plaza Costa Bavaro 809.996.1233 (recommended)

Indian

Pranama — Plaza El Dorado, Los Corales 809.552.6767 (recommended)

Mediterranean

Garum – San Juan Shopping Center 809.466.0505

Mediterraneo – Eden Roc at Cap Cana 809.469.7469

Latin American

Rancho Paisa – Plaza Mayoral, Bavaro 809.552.1895

Sea Food

Acqua Beach Club – Bibijagua, Bavaro Beach 809.552.6002

Capitan Cook – El Cortecito, Bavaro 809.552.1061

Jellyfish – Playa Bavaro 809.868.3040 (recommended)

La Yola – Punta Cana Resort & Club

809.959.2262

Oasis Montreal — El Cortecito, Bavaro

<u>Tips</u>

Mangu: Traditional Dominican morning favorite, made up of boiled green plantains. The plantains are then mashed with the water it has been boiling in. It is topped with sauteed onions and served with salami, deepfried cheese, fried eggs or avocado on the side.

Mofongo: You simply cannot leave without trying this! Green plantains are fried and mashed with garlic and fried pork rind. A true delicacy!

La Bandera (The Flag): The most popular of the national dishes, "la bandera" consists of a stewed meat dish, white rice, red kidney beans, fried plantains and salad and is served as lunch.

Wedding

Why do people plan weddings in Punta Cana? Punta Cana has become the perfect choice for a wedding for many reasons, but perhaps the most overwhelming is the breathtaking scenery. There are endless golden beaches that nestle up to the crisp azure waters of the ocean and there are also stunning colorful plants and flowers around every bend that will take your breath away. This is a laidback exciting way to start off the new chapter of your lives as a couple and it also creates a little minivacation for you and all of your guests as well. A conventional wedding costs a fortune. By the time you invite the hundreds of guests, pay for the church, dinner, entertainment and whatever else, you have spent tens of thousands of dollars. Weddings in Punta Cana have the potential to create a much more memorable experience and possibly save you lots of money. You will spend few days in paradise with your closest group of friends and say "I do" with the Caribbean as your backdrop, the memories of a lifetime!

Now planning your own Punta Cana wedding is quite easy because most of the work is going to be done by the wedding coordinators; of course, that doesn't mean you can completely forget about everything but it will certainly reduce the workload significantly. The big dilemma is always the choice of the location. Finding the perfect spot to get married in Punta Cana can be a bit challenging when it comes to planning a destination wedding.

All inclusive resorts have always been classic locations for destination weddings. Right now the most popular seem to be Majestic Colonial,

Majestic Elegance, Excellence, Dreams Punta Cana and Ocean Blue and Sand. However, specially in the last few years, more and more brides are choosing to set up the wedding reception offresort because they want do something (more) special for their Big Day. Here below is a list of the top 3 wedding receptions you can arrange offresort.

Jellyfish

Jellyfish restaurant in Punta Cana is right on the beach between the resorts Melia Caribe Tropical and IFA Villas Bavaro. Coming by car or taxi it's a 5 minute bumpy ride from the main road. But once you get there you'll see it's well worth the journey. The restaurant's architecture is unique. Set on 2 floors with a main dining area downstairs and a lounge upstairs both offer panoramic views over the white sand, palm trees and turquoise sea. Jellyfish is beautiful by day but by night the restaurant takes on an amazingly romantic ambiance. In fact it's probably the most popular offresort wedding venue in Punta Cana. They host hundreds of wedding ceremonies and dinner parties.

Cuisine: Seafood

Huracan Cafe'

Located in the Los Corales area, Huracan Cafe is one of the best places in the Dominican Republic to enjoy traditional Italian cuisine and international music. Typical dishes include such things as Huracan Fettucini, Penne Vodka and Seafood, Mozzarella in Carrozza. There is also an extensive wine list with many great Italian wines such as Pinot Grigio and Chianti. With its fantastic beachfront location, Huracan Cafe offers not only great cuisine, but also delicious Caribbean cocktails. At night the dining experience at Huracan Café becomes magical with the sound of the sea in the background and with the light of the full moon. Here excellent grilled meat and fresh fish can be enjoyed by candlelight on the beach, accompanied by live music and the best national and international DJs. Huracan Cafe offers great services to help guests celebrate events, specially weddings. Everything is done with all of the usual professionalism that has made Huracan Cafe what it is today.

Cuisine: Italian

Kukua Beach Club

Kukua Beach is a beautiful Beach Club located on the extraordinary beach of Arena Gorda. The Kukua Beach Club is described as a "place with soul". A dreamful environment, a magic setting that invites to relax and enjoy with all your senses. In addition to being one of the most visited and highly rated restaurants in Punta Cana, they can plan and host your dream wedding while you destress in their world class Kukua spa. Their specialties are the sea food platter, lobster and paella. The restaurants has also a private pool and a beautiful and unique private room for the bride.

Cuisine: Sea Food

Punta Cana is one of the most popular wedding directions in the world! We work with experienced wedding providers, who offer high quality of service more than 5 years in DR and have Englishspeaking masters of ceremonies.

Sports and Activities

Golf
Punta Cana District has ten 18hole golf courses and two 9hole golf courses in operation: Green Fees shown include transportation to and from your resort to the course as well as other inclusions such as a golf cart. Almost all golf courses includes club house, pro shop, bar and golf school. Golf carts mandatory. Fast greens, paspalum grass, whitesand bunkers, wide fairways and finegravel outofbounds. Must take into consideration strong breezes in oceanfront golf courses.

Barcelo: first ever, built in 1991 and redesigned by P.B. Dye last year inside Barcelo Bavaro Beach

Resort. $130. per round, special offers to guests of the Barcelo Bavaro Beach Resort. Driving and putting ranges.

Iberostate Golf Course: A beautiful P.B. Dye design over rolling hills located in Iberostar Bávaro Golf & Spa Resort. Driving range.

Cocotal Golf & Country Club: a Pepe Ganzedo design with 27 holes located in front of the Melia International Resort. Driving and putting ranges. $156. per round

La Cana Golf Club: at Puntacana Resort & Club, P.B: Dye oceanfront designed in 2000. Green Fees from $140, $105 for guests. Transportation not included.

La Hacienda: a P.B. Dye design in Puntacana Resort & Club. Rolling hills and the tropical forest. Green fees from $140 per 18 holes.

Corales: an exclusive formembersonly Tom Fazio 18hole masterpiece design, ocean front. By invitation.

Catalonia Caribe Golf Club: two golf courses, 9 holes near of the sea in Cabeza de Toro at the Catalonia Bavaro Resort (eastbound Punta Cana), $136 depending in season. A second 18hole golf course in the coastal plains. Off season as low as $40 and $25 for residents. Special offers for clients of the Catalonia Bavaro Resort. A 9hole Pitch & Putt, also.

White Sands Golf Course: a 9hole for beginners course located in Bavaro, near of the Ocean Blue & Sands Resort, $118.

Punta Espada: top 5 star Jack Nicklaus's masterpiece course, Cap Cana, considered among the best 50 golf courses worldwide. $375 ($275 off season), bottled water included. Driving range.

Punta Blanca Golf Course: Nick Price design nearby the Bahia Principe Resort, $176. per round, special deals for clients of the Hotels Majestic, Barcelo Punta Cana Premium and Bahia Principe. Driving range.

Hard Rock Hotel Punta Cana: a Nicklaus' signature design over rolling hills near of the ocean. Some deep greens and narrow fairways cut through the tropical forest. Green fees from $150. Driving range.

Two more designer golf courses are under construction: Jack Nicklaus' Iguana Golf Course in

Cap Cana (southwest coast) and Nick Faldos' Rocoki, over the north coast.

Golf Courses

Golf lover? Punta Cana is known for having great allinclusive resorts and the most beautiful beach in the world, but a lot of people don't realize that Punta Cana golf courses are the best in the Caribbean. They are spectacular because of the scenery and because they have tracked down some of the best designers in the world to create them. Designers include: Pete Dye; Jack Nicklaus; P.B. Dye; Nick Faldo and Robert Trent Jones to name a few.

Punta Cana golf courses have definitely taken over in recent years and now Punta Cana is the hottest golf destination in the Caribbean. With 12 golf courses open and many more under construction, a golfing boom is definitely happening in Punta Cana.

Punta Espalda Golf Course

The green fees to play at Punta Espada are hefty, but hear us out before you write it off: This par72 course is a Jack Nicklaus signature course and the site of a PGA Champions Tour. It's one of the most gorgeous courses in Punta Cana, with winding pathways and a topnotch beach view. Plus your day rate includes the rental of a golf cart, driving range practice, a caddy, and two bottles of water. Jack Nicklaus has created the first course in the Dominican Republic entirely with Paspalum grass. Nicklaus says that this grass is the best choice as it is resistant to saltwater, heat and remains incredibly green and lush

The prestigious Punta Espada is the first of three courses for the Cap Cana resorts of Punta Cana

(Secrets Sanctuary Cap Cana, Caleton Club & Villas and the Golden Bear Lodge & Spa). Visit the course's website for tee times and prices.

La Cana Golf Course
La Cana Golf Course has Seashore Paspalum grass, four holes directly along the seafront, and plenty of prestige. Golf lovers like that it's not as crowded or expensive as Punta Espada, plus it's more scenic than Barceló Bávaro.

Previous guests also say La Cana's prices are somewhat reasonable, considering its breathtaking scenery. Add in the fact that you can opt for a discounted rate and just nine holes of golf, and La Cana is one of the better valued courses in the district. But it's also very popular, so you should consider reserving your teetime as much as two weeks in advance, especially during peak travel season.

La Cana Golf Course was designed by P.B. Dye and is located on the grounds of the Punta Cana Resort & Club. With seven of the holes at the Punta Cana Golf Course running directly along the shores of the Caribbean, you truly feel that you're playing a seafront course – the views are breathtaking! The course gives you an odd feeling of being at a tropical Pebble Beach. Prices vary for hotel guests and outside players, the number of holes and equipment rental. Visit the hotel's website for more information on the course.

Corales Golf Club
Designed by Tom Fazio and opened in 2010, Corales is an exclusive and dramatic 18hole course with six Caribbean Oceanside holes. Designed along the natural cliffs, bays, ocean coves and the inland lakes and coralina quarries,

Corales Golf Course rates among the World's finest Golf Experiences. The exhilarating challenge culminates playing the Devil's Elbow, Corales's last three holes. The Devil's Elbow features the striking eighteenth hole with a dramatic forced carry over the cliff lined Bay of Corales, an inspired capstone to a memorable and breathtaking golf experience.

Barcelo' Bavaro The Lakes Golf Course
Designed by architect Juan Manuel Gordillo, this par72 course is one of the most popular spots to tee off in Punta Cana. Recent guests of the hotel and the course say the only real downside to Barceló Bávaro's 18 holes is that they aren't situated near the ocean. Until Dec. 24 this golf course will be renovating its front nine holes; visitors can play the back nine twice.

The greenway is located on the grounds of the Barceló Bávaro Beach Golf & Casino Resort, but open to outside guests as well. Day rates include equipment rental and hotel access, but you should make your reservations up to 24 hours in advance. Visit Bávaro's website for more information.

The Cocotal Golf Club

One of several resort style courses that were designed with the tourist in mind. It is designed by the Spanish golf champion, Joe Gancedo. The course consists of three 9 hole courses or 27 holes. The course features abundant vegetation and many water hazards for a challenging round on a beautiful and well maintained These courses tend to be enjoyable and somewhat forgiving, lending themselves to an under five hour round by tourists renting clubs. Cocotal Golf club is a lot of fun as it weaves through Coconut trees and small lakes, but is not a seafront course. You should probably tee off early if you want to avoid the busy time of day. course.

Iberostate Bavaro Golf & Club

The Iberostate Bavaro Golf Club is an island course located in the Iberostate residential development inside the Iberostar resort complex. The new Iberostate Bávaro Golf Club was carefully designed by P.B. Dye, working closely with stone and rock. The lush landscaping features many trees and palms, and includes roughs with native grasses. His finishing touch was guiding the course along the coast, where golfers of all handicaps will be able to enjoy both the scenery and the game.

This course is what resort golfing is all about a great round of golf while on vacation. Large mounds, small greens, hidden lakes and bunkers are the challenge, but its short length helps the less experienced golfers. The 16th hole is a signature par 3 with a small lake between the tee and green with a forest as a backdrop.

Cana Bay Palace – Hard Rock Golf Club
The Hard Rock Golf Club at Cana Bay hosts 18 holes of championship golf designed by Nicklaus Design. From the championship tees, it plays 7,253 yards and winds through native areas, exposed sand and rock. The course is seeded with paspalum turf from tee to green and plays firm and fast with small, sloping greens that make for difficult approach shots. A Par 72 course that provides a stunning collection of challenging yet accommodating golf for all players, regardless of skill level or experience. The course meanders through breathtaking

Dominican landscapes full of native flora and fauna.

Punta Blanca Golf Course

The Punta Blanca Golf Course is part of the five star Majestic Colonial Punta Cana Beach Resort. Located in the area of Punta Cana/Bavaro, Punta Blanca was designed by world renowned golf player Nick Price. The course plays through natural wetland areas with large waste bunkers and big lakes naturally built into the tropical vegetation. Opened in 2007, Punta Blanca is a magnificent inland golf course which should appeal to golfers of all levels even if the course if full of obstacles that will challenge even the most experienced golfers.

Roco Ki Golf Club – The Faldo Legacy Course

The Faldo Legacy golf course is the first to come online in Roco Ki with two more golf courses slated for the future. The Faldo Legacy Golf Course at Roco Ki has garnered high acclaim indeed from the Association of British Travel Agents who praised The Faldo Legacy Course at Roco Ki as one of the world's top 10 best new resorts, courses and projects for 2008. This is the first golf course in the Caribbean designed by Nick Faldo, the 2008 Ryder Cup captain.

Catalonia Caribe Golf Club
This 18 hole Par 72 course is the design of Alberto Sola, with the cooperation of Corrie Jack; the basic characteristic of this course, which counts on one of its greens within an artificial lake, is its horizontal amplitude. Five lagoons and trees define this small but challenging course. Designed as much for the experienced golfer as the beginner. It has ample fairways and keeps with the natural landscape. Despite being one of

the cheaper courses in the Bávaro area the Catalonia Caribe Golf Course is still in good shape with some interesting holes along the way. Also the maintenance standard of this course is surprisingly good considering the price compared to some of the areas other on more expensive golf courses. Especially the greens are in excellent conditions.

Snorkeling

Punta Cana features the longest coral reef on the whole island about 30 kilometers long.
Snorkeling from Shore is limited at all resorts to the marked swimming areas due to heavy all day long boat traffic(only exception is the boat traffic free Catalonia Royal Beach section), decent at select areas near the reef. Snorkeling excursions take groups to a area in front of the Melia Resort

and mostly to the prepared and secure snorkel sites in the Cabeza de Toro area, nice wide shallows full of fishes. a smaller shallow is also located near the Club Med on the Punta Cana side, top snorkel area is the huge wide and all around the year calm shallow at the Catalonia Bavaro Resort in Cabeza de Toro, specially the boat traffic free side of the Catalonia Royal Beach section, of course accessable for the public, this is the snorkel area from the beach, no boat ride/excursion needed.

Scuba

Diving is good, not great, because right in front of the Beaches Punta Cana is protected by a closed Barrier Reef. The area though is most appropriate for beginning divers. It is a great place to learn since the waters near to shore offer shallow beginner friendly dives full of smaller colored reef fishes/spezies. Excursions will take you to discover a shipwreck and lots of nice coral formations, channels and tunnels..

If you are serious about scuba diving, but still want to vacation in the Punta Cana area you may participate in dive excursions to Catalina Island, a 90 minutes drive away, the 2 top dives there are named the "Aquarium" and the "Wall", great diving sites, for acompaning nondivers great snorkeling is also available there. These dives are attractive to both beginners and advanced scuba divers.

Fishing

In this region, big game fishing is very good and annual tournaments draw international participants in the summer. Punta Cana counts within the world's Top 5 Destinations in case of the Famous White Marlin Fishing with it's peak season late Marchend June. You can look forward to catching blue marlin, white marlin, dorado(mahi), wahoo, yellowfin tunas, bonitos, barracudas and others. Best fishing is the long lasting Billfish season end March til end September. Arrangements can be made at the Marinas Cabeza de Toro, Punta Cana and Cap Cana, the still only secure and professional operating Marinas on the Dominican East Coast. the professional operating Marinas also started to offer their services with a few touroperators and at the guest services of some hotels. just make always sure that you really get contacted/hooked up by a fully insured Outfitter operating at a real Marina. end May 2009 the German Big Game Championship will be held in Cabeza de Toro.

Horseback riding

Several Ranches are located in the Punta Cana/Bavaro for all tastes and price ranges. In Punta Cana itself you have PUNTACANA Ranch which belong to PUNTACANA Resort & Club. The horses here are well taken care of and for beginner or advanced riders alike and all groups are always accompanied by 2 guides. The rides go down to the beach and through part of the gated community, offering a bit of everything and for all tastes.

Surfing

There is a Surf Camp operating in Macao Beach, one of the most beautiful beaches in the Punta Cana area; you can get Surfing lessons or rent a surfboard. MACAO SURF CAMP is run by Surfers with more than 30 years of experience, and really help you to learn this extreme sport as safe as possible, and if you already know you can rent a surfboard and even receive some coaching from the experts. Macao is a beach break with different "peaks" and you can ride left and right waves, when the wind is offshore you can ride very nice tubes.

Places with Free Wifi (OffResort)

A couple of good places to go for wireless internet are Las Lenas, a coffee shop in town, beside the Texaco and also at the Bamboo Bar and Soles, which are two restaurant/bars on the beach in Los Corales near the RE/MAX office.

Most resorts will provide wifi or internet facilities, usually for a small charge.

There's also an unlimited paid option from gobecon.com and the company has been gertting rave reviews. It's $29 a week and works everywhere.

For free wifi off the resort: (keep in mind that in most places a password is required...please ask)

In Cortecito:

- Chez Mon Ami in the Plaza Nautica

- Noir Beach Lounge on the beach between Carabella Bavaro Beach Resort and Grand Palladium Royal Suites Turquesa.

- Palma Sands on the beach 1 minute walk north of Noir Beach Lounge

- Photo Bar on the beach 1 min walk north of Palma Sands

Los Corales is the residential and shopping area stretching inland between NH Real Arena Resort and Barcelo Dominican Beach Resort. Free wifi can be found at:

- Dannys Sports Bar

- Soles Bar & Bamboo Bar both on the beach.

- D'Angelos Pizza/Cafe 3 minute walk inland

- New York Bakery/Cafe 6 minute walk inland

Palma Real Shopping Centre on the main road next to the entrance to Melia Caribe Tropical Resort & Paradisius Palma Real:

- Hard Rock Cafe

- Akai Sushi

- Tangerirne

- Tony Romas

- Mail Boxes Etc (using their computers)

Other wifi connections:

- Steve's Corner Bar in Plaza Punta Cana

- Jelly Fish Restaurant on the beach between Melia Caribe Tropical and IFA Villas Bavaro

- Acqua Beach Club on the beach just south of IFA Villas Bavaro

- Brot Cafe in PuntaCana Village opposite the airport

Rums

There are rums in literally all countries of the world, but only one place to find genuine Dominican rum! And that is right here! There are 6 major prodcers of rum and some lesser known operations. Most common to any part of the country are the products of Brugal, Barcelo and Bermudez. Along with the multiple bottles they produce, other quality brands include Macorix, Siboney and Don Rhum. In this counrty...if they sell water...they sell rum, and if they don't sell water...not to worry...they still sell rum!

Rums such as Macorix 8 year, Bermudez 1852 and Don Armando as well as Don Rhum come in boxes that make transporting back home much more convenient, as well as looking better when presenting a bottle as a gift.

Prices for rum vary, often most expensive at resort gift shops and areas supported by tourism. Cheapest locations are often at a Super Mercado (Super Market) or Colmado (Corner Store), but for many, this requires a taxi ride to get to. Waiting until you get to the airport is often your most expensive option when it comes to rum.

There is a rum refered to as Dominican gasoline....most notible by it's 151 labeling. This is about as much alcohol as you are going to find in a bottle. Not particularly great tasting, its ability to render you a babbling idiot is what it is all about! One warning though...most airlines will not allow 151 onboard regardless of its checked lugguage or not.

Also, when it comes to transporting rum back home, please remember to pack your purchases in you checked lugguage...not your carry on. The will not permit you to take it onboard.

Many of the rums sold, come in smaller bottles as well, making it easy to sample a bottle without wasting any! Nothing worse than spending money on something you simply do not like!

North Coast

In Sosua at Super Super Liquors at the corner of Pedro Clisante and Ayuntamiento streets has the best prices in town. The Brugal factory is located in the east end of the city and is a major tourist attraction.

East Coast

Punta Cana / Bavaro, offers no shortage of opportunities to buy rum. If you wish to save a buck, supermercados are the places to be, but keep in mind, most will require an expensive cab ride, thus you should factor that into your purchases. Cheapest prices and best selection can be found at Super Mercado Estrella located on what many refer to as Friusa.

School Visits

Many tourists like to visit the schools in the Punta Cana area a/d or make donations of school supplies.

Often, these schools prefer that visitors come to the schools after 3 pm as not to disrupt the classes. School supplies are in short supply and they are gratefully accepting all donations of supplies. Please do not take cash as they have no way of providing proof of what they purchased and do not want to be susceptible to any fraudulent accusations.

Beyond the Beach Children's Foundation (info@beyondthebeach.ca) does not like to see children begging, thus have setup a distribution network to get supplies, clothes and donations to the needy in many regions of the Dominican Republic.have setup people in the different areas to accept donations on behalf of the foundation and they will see that it gets to the right people. On the website, you can click on the area you are visiting and you will find contact information there.

Keep in mind that BTBCF does not bring visitors along when dropping off donations/supplies at the schools and does he arrange such visits. Only goods accepted are accepted for direct donations; cash donations should be made to the Foundation.

Hotels in Punta Cana

Holidays in Punta Cana depend on what category of hotel you choose and how many days will last your vacation. It is considered one of the best resorts in the Dominican Republic, and located on the southeast of the country. Resort is famous for its beaches, the best in the country. White sand, forest of coconut palms, which stretches for miles, crystal clear water, tranquil lagoon, protected from ocean waves by a coral reef, luxury hotels of Punta Cana and excellent service. The name of the resort is translated as "a meeting place of all palms", and it speaks for itself so many palm trees are found nowhere else in the world.

The town of Punta Cana is not rich in the historical past: the first settlements began to appear here about 30 years ago. At that time the resort was a desert with a jungle of mangrove trees and palms. For two decades the town has become a prestigious resort, which is considered the best in the entire country. During this time, among the palms and mangrove trees have grown about 30 different hotels. It is noteworthy, that the residents of the city are trying to follow a single "tropical" style in the construction of the buildings, using bamboo and palm trees.

Punta Cana is famous for its fourand fivestar hotels, which offer many services under the program "all inclusive". The cost of accommodation at the hotel typically includes daily entertainments in the evenings, drinks and cocktails in the bar, disco, table games and the use of nonmotorized boats, sports hall and three meals a day. Punta Cana hotels are of the different areas: some have focused on the possibilities of sport, while others are designed for a family holidays. Most of them are placed along the cost line, and there are no practically small hotels. Visit once Punta Cana and you will remember it for life. Being at home, you will long be under the impressions of this beautiful paradise, where you spend an unforgettable time. And on winter evenings, reviewing a stack of photos from vacation, you will want to return to this wonderful place.

We offer 1400 hotels in Punta Cana Dominican Republic with low prices and discount rates. Our reservation system features cheap and luxury hotels in Punta Cana, hostels, motels, B&B and other affordable accommodations in Punta Cana. We have great hotel deals in central Punta Cana. You can also book Punta Cana airport hotels at cheap rates. Our system is secure and absolutely free of charge.

Apartments

Stanza Mare, Bavaro Beach, Dvr

Stanza Mare, Bavaro Beach, Dvr Punta Cana, situated in Bavaro district, 1.9 km from Dolphin Island Park, boasts a sun deck, barbeque and an indoor swimming pool. The accommodation offers rooms with air conditioner, an iron/ironing board and a private safe as well as a kitchen.

The apartment lies within a 25minute walk of Yacht & catamaran sailing. The private beach is 150 metres away. Soles Chill Out Bar as a dining option is approximately 350 metres away. Take a few minutes' cab ride to see Cortecito Beach.

The property features beautiful rooms with views of the sea. Hypoallergenic pillows and linens as well as hair dryers, bath sheets and a separate shower are included in the rooms. The venue is equipped with an en suite bathroom with a shower and a walkin shower.

The units at Stanza Mare, Bavaro Beach, Dvr apartment have an electric kettle, an oven, coffee and tea making facilities. Punta Cana airport can be accessed in 25 minutes by car. You can engage in various activities, such as snorkelling, fishing services and diving organised by the property.

Checkin:from 15:0020:00 hours

Checkout:until 09:0011:00 hours

- Children and extra beds

- All children under the age of 13 may stay free of charge when using existing beds.

- One child under the age of 3 may stay for free in an extra bed.

Presidential Suites Punta Cana

Offering an outdoor swimming pool, a swimming pool and a bar, Presidential Suites Punta Cana is 25 minutes' walk from Cortecito Beach. Situated in Bavaro district, the venue is set 2.1 km from Palma Real Shopping Village.

The accommodation lies near the sand beach. A beautiful beach is 5 minutes' walk from the hotel. Presidential Suites is a short ride from Casino Diamante Punta Cana Grand.

The comfortable rooms come with coffee/tea making facilities, climate control, iron and ironing board, while a microwave oven, a freezer and a fullsized fridge are also at guests' disposal. Some of the airconditioned units have views of the ocean. A hairdryer, towels and bath sheets are featured.

A buffet breakfast is served every morning in restaurant at Presidential Suites. Guests can enjoy Central American and Venezuelan meals at Living Room within 5 minutes' walk of the property. There are facials and a spa therapy provided free of charge. It offers a spa salon with various massages, a wellness area and a sauna. Onsite you can engage in various activities, such as kayaking and lawn tennis.

Checkin:from 15:0023:59 hours

Checkout:until 11:00 hours

Children and extra beds

All children under the age of 4 may stay free of charge when using existing beds.

All children under the age of 11 may stay at the price of us$ 50 per person per night in an extra bed.

There are no cots provided in a room.

Terraza Art Villa Dominicana Punta Cana

Terraza Art Villa Dominicana Punta Cana is set 0.2 km from Plaza Turquesa and 1.5 km from Dolphin Island Park in Bavaro district. Ironing, laundry and 24hour security are provided onsite, while a garden, a golf course and a sundeck are also available.

The accommodation is near Supermercado Ciccolella and just a stroll from parks. The beaches of Punta Cana are about 650 metres away. Sweet Coffee and Garota Rodizio & Grill are within 5 minutes' walk of the apartment. Manatee Park is also a short ride away.

A separate toilet, a TV set and cable channels are featured in the rooms. Guests staying at this apartment have access to a terrace. This property comprises 1 airconditioned bedroom.

Towels, bath sheets and showers are also provided.

Kitchen amenities feature kitchenware, refrigerator and a microwave. Punta Cana airport is 20 km away from the apartment. Terraza Art Villa Dominicana apartment invites you to relax with a bar, a sun deck and a summer terrace.

Checkin:from 14:0023:59 hours

Checkout:until 12:00 hours

Children and extra beds

There are no cots provided in a room.

The Sanctuary @ Los Corales Apartment Punta Cana

The Sanctuary @ Los Corales apartment is situated in Bavaro district of Punta Cana and provides accommodation with an outdoor swimming pool, a plunge pool and a free carpark. The venue comes with a yearround outdoor pool and is set 1.4 km from Cocotal Golf and Country Club.

Located not far from the Stunning Los Corales WhiteSand Beach Bavaro, the property is 800 metres from a private beach. A 10minute drive from the property leads to Seaquarium Punta Cana. Guests can go out for a meal to the pizzeria La Piazzetta Trattoria Pizzeria. Dolphin Island Park is set at a short driving distance.

The apartment is equipped with a personal safe, a seating area and multichannel television and a kitchen with tea and coffee making facilities, kitchenware, and refrigerators. This venue offers 6 rooms. A hairdryer, bath sheets and towels are provided upon request.

The nearest airport is Punta Cana set 25 km away. During your stay you can rent cars and bicycles.

Checkin:from 16:0023:30 hours

Checkout:until 08:0011:00 hours

Children and extra beds

There are no extra beds provided in a room.

Punta Cana Bavaro Suites Pool

Situated 1.8 km from Dolphin Island Park, Punta Cana Bavaro Suites Pool apartment provides accommodation with free WiFi throughout the venue. A kitchen with a fridge and toaster will add comfort to your stay.

The property is located in Bavaro district of Punta Cana, a 24minute drive from Punta Cana airport. Palma Real Shopping Village is 2.2 km from the apartment. Several restaurants such as Batu Music And Sport Bar and D'Angelo's Pizza & Pasta are within 250 metres from Punta Cana Bavaro Suites Pool apartment. Manatee Park can be reached in a few minutes by car.

Rooms include such amenities as air conditioner, a separate toilet and a dressing room. Down pillows, linens and feather pillows as well as towels, a hairdryer and bath sheets are included in the rooms. There is a shower and a walkin shower in a bathroom.

Guests can dive into an outdoor swimming pool. Such children facilities as children's menu and a special menu are provided onsite. Other facilities offered at the property include a nightclub, a bar and a sunbathing terrace.

Checkin:from 07:0023:59 hours

Checkout:until 07:0014:00 hours

Everything Punta Cana Los Corales Apartment

Situated in Bavaro district, Everything Punta Cana Los Corales apartment has a saltwater swimming pool, an aqua park and a golf course. The Scenic Los Corales WhiteSand Beach Bavaro is a short walking distance away, while Manatee Park is just a few minutes' drive from this venue.

Palma Real Shopping Village is 2.6 km away, while Bavaro Beach is set 10 minutes by car. This property boasts direct access to the own beach. There are restaurants serving Italian and international specialities 150 metres from the accommodation.

Featuring a private safe, a flatscreen TV with satellite channels and an individual safe, the rooms also come with a shared lounge. The venue has 7 rooms. Guests can make use of a shower, dryers and bath sheets for no additional supplement.

The nearest airport is Punta Cana, 25 km from Everything Punta Cana Los Corales apartment. An outdoor pool can be found on the premises. A selection of activities is offered in the area, such as diving, hiking and bowling.

Checkin:from 15:0021:00 hours

Checkout:until 09:0011:00 hours

Children and extra beds

All children may stay at the price of us$ 10 per person per night in an extra bed.

There are no extra beds provided in a room.

Exclusive Residencial Nautilus Bavaro Punta Cana

Exclusive Residencial Nautilus Bavaro PuntaCana apartment is located within 15 minutes' walk of the vibrant Princess Tower Casino Punta Cana and features a sun deck, a sun terrace and an outdoor pool. The venue is a 10minute ride to Cana Bay Golf Course.

The property is located in Bavaro district of Punta Cana. The apartment is a 10minute walk from the restaurant Fuego Latin Fussion. Punta Blanca Golf Club is also a short ride away.

This accommodation a kitchenette, coffee and tea making facilities, and a dining area, in addition to a fully furnished kitchen for selfcatering purposes. A terrace is featured in certain rooms. Bath sheets, towels and a tub are provided in this venue.

You can also make use of a refrigerator, an oven and coffee/tea makers. Punta Cana airport can be reached in about 24 minutes by car. Guests can dive into an outdoor swimming pool. Some units include children's menu and a special menu. You can engage in various activities, such as diving, horseback riding and fishing.

Checkin:from 14:0018:00 hours

Checkout:until 08:0011:00 hours

Children and extra beds

There are no extra beds provided in a room.

There are no cots provided in a room.

Monkey Banana Bavaro Punta Cana Apartment

Featuring free WiFi throughout the property, Monkey Banana Bavaro Punta Cana apartment is situated in Punta Cana, 20 km from Punta Cana airport. There is also a minikitchen, equipped with an oven, coffee/tea makers and kitchenware in every unit.

Manatee Park is 4 km away and guests can drive to Dolphin Island Park in 5 minutes. The venue is a 5minute walk from the beach. Monkey Banana Bavaro Punta Cana apartment is set in Bavaro district, within about 5 minutes' walk of Da Vinci Restaurante and Rincon Sabroso Restaurant serving a range of dishes. CrossFit Punta Cana is a short walk away.

This accommodation will provide you with tea and coffee making facilities, flatscreen TV, and a kitchenette in the rooms. They are fitted with tile flooring. The property offers 2 bedrooms that sleep up to 4 guests. For your comfort, you will find bath sheets, towels and a drier.

A fitness area is available for active residents. You will also find a community pool, flat screen TV and an outdoor swimming pool on site.

Checkin:from 15:0023:00 hours

Checkout:until 08:0012:00 hours

Children and extra beds

There are no cots provided in a room.

Villa Blanca Punta Cana

Featuring free Wi Fi in the rooms, Blanca apartment is situated in Punta Cana, 15 km from Punta Cana airport. The venue is made up of 6 rooms.

The property is within 3.4 km of Seaquarium Punta Cana and about 4 km from Manatee Park. Guests can find Dolphin Island Park in the area. Serving a wide range of dishes, Huracan Cafe and Dulce Tentacion can be reached in 25 minutes' walk. This apartment is located within a few minutes' drive from Cortecito Beach.

This accommodation features a private safe, a personal safe and a safe. Such bathroom facilities as a shower, bath sheets and towels are provided for guests.

Some units also include a microwave oven, coffee & tea makers and kitchenware.

Checkin:from 15:0019:00 hours

Checkout:until 12:00 hours

Children and extra beds

All children under the age of 12 may stay at the

price of us$ 25 per person per night in an extra bed.

Older children/adults may stay at the price of us$ 25 per person per night in an extra bed.

Villas

Deluxe Villas Bavaro Beach & Spa

Best Price For Long Term Vacation Rental Punta Cana

This venue is located 0.4 km from the Scenic Los Corales WhiteSand Beach Bavaro and 4 km from Manatee Park. A kitchenette and climate control are featured in the rooms, while refrigerators, coffee/tea making machines and toaster are provided in a minikitchen.

Situated in Bavaro district, the accommodation right next to dominican fantasy and within a few minutes' drive to Splash Water Park. The villa is surrounded by palm trees and gardens. Soles Chill Out Bar and D'Angelo's Pizza & Pasta, serving different delicacies, are about 175 metres away. The property is near Dolphin Island Park in Punta Cana.

Punta Cana airport is situated approximately 25 km away. Guests can relax by an outdoor pool. The accommodation offers yoga classes and a gym area as well as a dance club available.

Checkin:from 14:0023:00 hours

Checkout:until 09:0012:00 hours

La Flor Del Caribe Villa Punta Cana

Los Corales 6, Bavaro, Punta Cana, Punta Cana, Dominican Republic

La Flor Del Caribe Villa is situated in proximity to Dolphin Island Park and offers a community pool, a tennis court and an outdoor pool. A private bathroom as well as a kitchen with coffee/tea making equipment, refrigerator and a microwave are at the guests' disposal.

Palma Real Shopping Village can be found at a 1.6 km distance from the venue and Splash Water Park is 7 km away. The closest beach is 50 metres away. D'Angelo's Pizza & Pasta can be found about 200 metres away and it serves Italian and international dishes. The Scenic Los Corales WhiteSand Beach Bavaro is nearby as well.

Rooms are fitted with a TV, a balcony and climate control. These airconditioned rooms offer terrace views and also feature hypoallergenic pillows and linens. A drier, a shower and guest toiletries are provided in this accommodation.

La Flor Del Caribe Villa is 25 km from Punta Cana airport. A special menu, children's menu and board games are arranged for guests with children. If you would like stay in shape, try diving, windsurfing and canoeing.

Checkin:from 14:3021:30 hours

Checkout:until 06:0012:00 hours

Villas Paseo Del Sol Punta Cana

Avenida Barcelo Ifa Villas Bavaro, Punta Cana, Dominican Republic
Villas Paseo Del Sol offers an accommodation within 20 minutes by car from Punta Cana airport. A balcony, a personal safe and a flatscreen TV with satellite channels are featured in rooms at this venue.

The vibrant Princess Tower Casino Punta Cana is 3.8 km from the villa. Guests can visit Manatee

Park, which is a 10minute drive from this property. You can get to ChocoMuseo Punta Cana in a few minutes by car.

Beds with linens and hypoallergenic pillows are available for use. The bathroom comes with a rollin shower, a shower and a sink and a hairdryer, a roll in shower and towels.

Selfcatering facilities include a washing machine, kitchenware, coffee and tea making facilities.

Checkin:from 15:0023:30 hours

Checkout:until 12:0013:00 hours

Children and extra beds

All children under the age of 6 may stay free of charge when using existing beds.

There are no cots provided in a room.

Beach Villas & Apartments Larimar Punta Cana

Calle Los Corales, Punta Cana, Dominican Republic

This Beach Villas & Apartments Larimar is located not far from Dolphin Island Park. A safe, a writing desk and a separate toilet are provided in the rooms, as well as coffee and tea making facilities, kitchenware, and glassware in a kitchen.

The venue is placed only 1.6 km from Palma Real Shopping Village and around 2.6 km away from Cortecito Beach. The closest beach is 850 metres away. Offering Italian and Caribbean meals, Huracan Cafe is around 250 metres away. The proximity to dominican fantasy is a perk for those staying at Beach Villas & Apartments Larimar.

Hypoallergenic pillows and linens are provided. Bathrooms are appointed with a hair dryer, bath sheets and towels.

The accommodation is about 26 minutes' drive from Punta Cana airport. The villa also offers children's menu and a special menu for guests with children. Onsite recreational facilities involve a golf course, a bar and an aqua park as well as a wellness area and a spa area.

Checkin:from 14:3021:30 hours

Checkout:until 08:0012:00 hours

Alex Villas Golf Resort Iberostate

Av. Estados Unidos, Punta Cana, Dominican Republic

This Alex Villas Golf Resort Iberostate is located not far from Iberostar Golf Course. Overlooking the garden, the accommodation features a kitchen with a microwave oven, a dishwasher and an electric kettle.

The venue is a 5minute drive from Punta Blanca Golf Club and a 10minute drive from Arena Gorda Beach. You can get to Cortecito Beach in a few minutes by car.

Alex Villas Golf Resort Iberostate offers rooms featuring a flatscreen TV with satellite channels, a private safe and air conditioner. Fitted with a patio, these rooms feature a shared bathroom with a roll in shower, showers and bath sheets. A bathroom with a shower, a walkin shower and a rollin shower is also provided.

Punta Cana airport is nearly 30 km away. Guests are free to use an aqua park, an outdoor pool area and a flat screen TV.

Checkin:from 16:0023:59 hours

Checkout:until 06:0012:00 hours

Children and extra beds

There are no cots provided in a room.

Resort Atlantic Villas & Spa Punta Cana

Paradise Street 2 (Calle Las Terrazza), Punta Cana, Dominican Republic
Resort Atlantic Villas & Spa in Bavaro district of Punta Cana offers an aqua park, a free car park and a wellness area as well as the access to El Cortecito, which is 900 metres away. This venue has bath sheets, showers and guest toiletries in a private bathroom and a kitchen is provided with kitchenware, a microwave and refrigerator.

The Scenic Los Corales WhiteSand Beach Bavaro is 550 metres from the accommodation, while Bavaro Beach is 3.2 km away. An own beach is within 10 minutes' walk away of the proeprty.

The nearby La Piazzetta Trattoria Pizzeria is 50 metres away. Dolphin Island Park is a walking distance from Resort Atlantic Villas & Spa.

Rooms in this accommodation are furnished with ironing facilities, a flatscreen TV with satellite channels and coffee/tea making facilities. The property features tiled floors in these rooms. Beds fitted with linens and hypoallergenic pillows are available.

Punta Cana airport is located 25 km away. Other amenities include board games, children's menu and a special menu for kids. Guests can relax with various massages, a wellness centre and a spa centre provided on site.

Checkin:from 14:3023:30 hours
Checkout:until 09:0012:00 hours

Children and extra beds

There are no extra beds provided in a room.

Tropical Villas Deluxe Beach & Spa Punta Cana

Arruba, Punta Cana, Dominican Republic
Guests of Punta Cana will enjoy their stay at Tropical Villas Deluxe Beach & Spa apartment. The venue comprises of 1 bedroom and a minikitchen.

Yacht & catamaran sailing is set 1.8 km from the Property, while Manati Park Bavaro is 4.3 km away. You can visit a park set close to the apartment. The venue lies in Bavaro district.BAM Market and Palma Real Shopping Village are both at hand.

It offers an accommodation with an inroom safe, a flatscreen television and a trouser press included in the rooms. This property can accommodate up to 2 guests. The apartment includes 1 bathroom.

Punta Cana (PUJPunta Cana Intl.) airport is a 20minute drive away.An outdoor pool can be found on the premises.

Checkin:from 15:0021:30 hours

Checkout:until 10:0012:00 hours

Children and extra beds

There are no cots provided in a room.

Villa Cocotal Palma Real Punta Cana

Cocotal Palma Real Villas Bavaro, Punta Cana, Dominican Republic

Situated in Bavaro district, Villa Cocotal Palma Real provides a sundeck, an outdoor swimming pool and a golf course at 4 km from Seaquarium Punta Cana. It also has 3 bedrooms as well as a kitchen which is equipped with glassware, refrigerators and kitchenware.

Yacht & catamaran sailing is approximately 10 minutes' drive away. You can get to Cortecito Beach in a few minutes by car.

Offering outdoor pool views, this accommodation will provide you with a separate toilet, a sofa and an adjoining terrace. It includes 3 bathrooms with a walkin shower, a shower and a bidet alongside with towels, hairdryers and bath sheets.

Punta Cana airport is within 23 minutes by car from the venue. At this villa, you will find a flat screen TV, a sun deck and a summer terrace.

Checkin:from 15:0023:59 hours
Checkout:until 12:00 hours

Children and extra beds

There are no cots provided in a room.

Beach Resort Caribbean White Sand & Ocean Punta Cana

Calle Aruba, Punta Cana, Dominican Republic
Featuring complimentary parking, a safety deposit box and a newspaper stand, Beach Resort Caribbean White Sand & Ocean offers accommodation in Bavaro district, 7 km from ChocoMuseo Punta Cana. The venue looks over the garden and has a spa with a spa centre and massage.

Dolphin Island Park is located near the hotel, and Punta Cana airport is appropximately a 20minute drive away. The distance to Manati Park Bavaro is about 4.3 km.In addition, Seaquarium Punta Cana is within a walking distance of the property.

Rooms have climate control, a safe and a coffee maker. All units feature a microwave oven, fridges and a toaster.

Serving a wide assortment of dishes, Wacamole, Dulce Tentacion and Santo Pez Cocina Del Mar are about 50 metres from the venue.

Checkin:from 14:0023:59 hours

Checkout:until 10:0012:00 hours

Children and extra beds

There are no extra beds provided in a room.

Hotels

Iberostar Punta Cana Hotel

Carretera Arena Gorda Playa Bávaro, Punta Cana, Punta Cana, Dominican Republic
Located within 25 minutes' walk of Iberostar Golf Course, the comfortable Iberostar Punta Cana Hotel features flat screen TV, an entertainment

programme and a garden. This venue offers accommodation in Bavaro district with nearby access to Plaza Punta Cana.

This hotel is also 2 km from Splash Water Park. The property places you within 0.2 km of Playa Arena Gorda. Arena Gorda Beach is just a few minutes' drive away.

You can enjoy cable TV, free WiFi and cable channels, featured in stylish rooms. Some of the airconditioned units have views of the garden. Sun loungers and parasols provided on the a private balcony will add more comfort to your stay.

Begin the day with buffet breakfast. Guests can enjoy alcoholic drinks at the lounge bar. The venue has a hot tub and a swimming pool offered for no fee. It has sauna facilities, various massages and a hairdressing salon to relax. Alternatively, you can unwind with sailing, archery and kayaking onsite or in the surrounding area.

Checkin:from 15:0023:59 hours

Checkout:until 12:00 hours

Children and extra beds

There are no cots provided in a room.

Hotel Riu Bambu Punta Cana

Playa Arena Gorda, Punta Cana, Dominican Republic

Featuring an outdoor pool area, a sundeck and a tennis court, Hotel Riu Bambu is 10 minutes' drive from the vibrant Princess Tower Casino Punta Cana. Arena Gorda Beach is less than 1.6 km away.

Featuring a sunbed and lounge chairs, the sandy beach is just 500 metres away. The venue is directly on the beach. Punta Blanca Golf Club is only a short drive away.

The rooms offer WiFi, cable satellite TV and a private safe as well as guest bathrooms. Nice touches include showers, a bathtub and hair dryers.

A continental breakfast is served in the morning in the restaurant. There is a poolside bar onsite. This beachfront accommodation is less than 30 km from Punta Cana airport. A swimming pool and a Jacuzzi are provided free of charge for your convenience. Guests at Hotel Riu Bambu can enjoy an outdoor swimming pool. This property is a perfect place to practise lawn tennis, beach volleyball and pingpong.

Checkin:from 14:0023:59 hours

Checkout:until 12:00 hours

Riu Palace Bavaro Hotel Punta Cana

Playa De Arena Gorda, Punta Cana, Dominican Republic

Riu Palace Bavaro Hotel Punta Cana is 2 km from Arena Gorda Beach and features tennis courts, an outdoor pool area and a sun deck. Punta Blanca Golf Club is less than 2.5 km away.

This venue enjoys its beachfront location in vicinity of Splash Water Park. At this accommodation you'll be in 5 minutes' walk from Playa Arena Gorda. Cana Bay Golf Course is only a couple of minutes' drive away.

This establishment offers free WiFi, highvelocity internet and satellite TV in airconditioned rooms.

For your comfort, you will find a drier, a hairdryer and guest toiletries.

A continental breakfast is served every morning in restaurant at Riu Palace Bavaro Hotel. Guests can try soft drinks in the swimup bar where billiards table, a spacious terrace and a lounge await them too. There are facials and a spa therapy provided free of charge. You will enjoy a swimming pool, a gym facility as well as a Turkish steam bath, a spa centre and steam baths. For exercise, Riu Palace Bavaro Hotel offers aqua fitness and fitness centre.

Checkin:from 14:0023:59 hours

Checkout:until 12:00 hours

Grand Sirenis Punta Cana Resort & Aquagames

Playa De Uvero Alto, Punta Cana, Dominican Republic

Featuring a tennis court, a wellness centre and a nightclub, Grand Sirenis Punta Cana Resort & Aquagames offers accommodation in Uvero Alto district, 1.6 km from Carretera Uvero Alto Route. A poolside bar as well as an aqua park, an outdoor pool area and a bar can be enjoyed at the property, boasting the setting next to Sirenis Aquagames Punta Cana.

The venue is located in the tourist district of Punta Cana. Playa Uvero Alto Shopping Mall is settled 10 minutes' drive from the resort. El Merengue is within walking distance of this luxurious hotel.

The rooms offered here are individual and include satellite television, wireless Internet, tea and coffee making equipment. Some of the airconditioned units have views of the outdoor pool. For your comfort, you will find a hairdryer, complimentary toiletries and a dryer.

Try the hotels' daily buffet breakfast available in the restaurant. The menu of Cinecitta restaurant offers dishes of Italian cuisine. Enjoy billiards, WiFi and a TV in the Beach bar. Punta Cana airport is within 45 km. Guests can make use of free leisure facilities including a swimming pool and a spa therapy. Grand Sirenis Punta Cana Resort & Aquagames provides a spa centre, massage and facials. A gym offers fitness classes and aerobics classes.

Checkin:from 15:0023:59 hours

Checkout:until 11:0012:00 hours

Children and extra beds

Maximum capacity of extra beds in a room is 1.

Barcelo Bavaro Palace All Inclusive (Adults Only)

Carretera Bavaro Km 1, Bavaro, Dominican Republic

Barcelo Bavaro Palace All Inclusive Punta Cana offers exquisite accommodation close to Dolphin Island as well as a summer terrace, a nightclub and a sun deck. The venue is 1.8 km from Bibijagua, while Dolphin Explorer Seaside Park is 4.5 km away.

The hotel lies near the white beach. A 10minute walk will bring you to a pristine beach. Cabeza de Toro Beach is a few minutes' drive away.

Modern rooms are fully equipped with wireless internet, free wireless internet and satellite television, also offering tea/coffee making equipment, a microwave oven and a fridge for selfcatering. Jacuzzi provided on the a private balcony will add more comfort to your stay.

Try the hotels' daily buffet breakfast available in the restaurant. Guests can enjoy a drink in the café bar which features a spacious terrace, billiards table and a lounge. Santa Fe Steak House and Kyoto Japanese Restaurant & Sushi Bar are an 8minute walk away, and they offer some of the best cuisine in Punta Cana. The property boasts a tennis court and a gym free of charge. Relaxation at Barcelo Bavaro Palace All Inclusive is provided at facials, steam baths and a wellness area. Guests can relax in an outdoor swimming pool or enjoy aqua fitness, aerobics classes and fitness centre.

Checkin:from 15:0023:59 hours
Checkout:until 12:00 hours

Children and extra beds

All children under the age of 2 may stay free of charge when using existing beds.

Maximum capacity of extra beds in a room is 1.

Riu Naiboa Hotel Punta Cana

Playa Arena Gorda, Punta Cana, Dominican Republic

Riu Naiboa Hotel Punta Cana is located 2.5 km from Iberostar Golf Course and offers 24hour security, 24 hour front desk assistance and concierge service. Arena Gorda Beach is less than 2.3 km away.

The beach is just 850 metres away with sun loungers and chaise loungers available. It is also within 11 minutes' walk of the sandy beach. Splash Water Park is also located near the venue. The accommodation is set next to Splash Water World.

The property features flatscreen TV, free WiFi and television in the guest rooms. A hair dryer, a tub and showers are provided.

Guests of Riu Naiboa Hotel will enjoy a daily cold buffet breakfast during their stay. You can select refreshing drinks served at the lounge bar. Steam baths and facials are available and free of charge. It offers a sauna with massage treatments, a wellness area and a Jacuzzi. Guests can make use of the gym, fitness classes and fitness studio.

Checkin:from 14:0023:59 hours

Checkout:until 12:00 hours

Bahia Principe Grand Aquamarine (Adults Only)

Arena Gorda, Punta Cana, Dominican Republic

Located within 15 minutes' walk of Punta Blanca Golf Club, the beachfront Bahia Principe Grand Aquamarine Hotel Punta Cana features an outdoor pool area, a swimming pool and water slides. Boasting location close to Arena Gorda Beach, the venue offers views of the Atlantic Ocean along with massage, a solarium and a wellness area onsite.

The accommodation is set about 7 minutes' walk from the white beach. It is also just a 10 minutes' drive from Splash Water Park. Bahia Principe Grand Aquamarine Hotel is a short ride from Iberostar Golf Course.

Airconditioned rooms include highvelocity internet, ironing facilities and wireless Internet as well as a pillowtop mattress and linens. For your comfort, you will find here coffee & tea making facilities and glassware.

Try the hotels' daily buffet breakfast available in the restaurant. Guests can try alcoholic drinks in the swimup bar where live music, a spacious terrace and a casino await them too. Punta Cana airport is in 32 minutes by car. Live performances and karaoke are offered too. Daytime activities for adults include fitness classes and aerobics classes.

Checkin:from 15:0023:59 hours

Checkout:until 12:00 hours

Children and extra beds

There are no extra beds provided in a room.

Riu Palace Macao (Adults Only) Hotel Punta Cana

Located 1.6 km from Arena Gorda Beach, guests of 4star Riu Palace Macao Hotel Punta Cana may find tennis courts, a golf course and a community pool onsite. The venue is placed next to sand beaches.

This accommodation is in a 12minute walk from Splash Water Park. The property places you within 0.3 km of Playa Arena Gorda. Riu Palace Macao Hotel is a short ride from Astron.

The hotel's rooms include WiFi, a personal safe and an adjoining terrace. Guests can also make use of a hairdryer, a spa bathtub and dressing gowns.

The property features a continental breakfast in the restaurant. Finish the evening in the poolside bar with refreshing drinks. The venue is located close to a ship terminal. This impressive venue offers steam baths and a spa therapy free of charge. Guests can reenergize with a spa area, a hot tub and sauna facilities available on site. There are fitness classes and a fitness studio located in different parts of the hotel.

Checkin:from 14:0023:59 hours

Checkout:until 12:00 hours

Four Points By Sheraton Hotel Punta Cana

Boulevard 1Ero De Noviembre, Punta Cana, Dominican Republic

Being set in the very heart of Punta Cana, close to PUNTACANA Village, Four Points By Sheraton Hotel offers tennis courts, a bar and an outdoor pool area. Guests have access to a swimming pool, a gym facility and free Wi Fi in public areas.

Corales Golf Course is 3.7 km from the venue and Marina Cap Cana is 7 km away. The accommodation is located close to own beach. Four Points By Sheraton Hotel is a short driving distance of Playa Blanca Beach.

The rooms are comfortable and come with WiFi, cable television and cable channels as well as private bathrooms. They have a modernstyle interior.

Guests can have breakfast in the restaurant every morning. The resort features Ara restaurant. A setting near a motorway offers good public transport connections. A fitness centre and a spa therapy can be provided at a surcharge. Four Points By Sheraton Hotel offers options for sports and relaxation in massage treatments, a spa centre and a wellness area or at fitness studio and fitness classes. Guests can also enjoy diving, snorkelling and fishing services.

Checkin:from 15:0023:59 hours

Checkout:until 12:00 hours

Resorts

Barcelo Bavaro Palace All Inclusive Punta Cana

Playas De Bavaro, Punta Cana, Dominican Republic

An outdoor pool, a nightclub and a bar are offered at Barcelo Bavaro Palace All Inclusive Punta Cana, located 3.8 km from Cocotal Golf and Country Club. Situated in Bavaro district, the resort is set 1.1 km from Barcelo Golf Bavaro.

The venue lies near the private beach. The beach is 650 metres away. Barcelo Bavaro Palace All Inclusive is a short ride from Manatee Park.

Guests can choose from modern rooms with television and climate control. Complimentary toiletries, showers and slippers are featured.

Residents can have breakfast in the restaurant. Bohio Dominicano restaurant which serves local cuisine is great accommodation for a meal. The bar offers billiards and a spacious terrace as well as an array of selected drinks. A hot tub and a sauna are free for all guests at Barcelo Bavaro Palace All Inclusive. It features an outdoor swimming pool and a spa salon for your leisure time. Fitness classes and aerobics classes are possible in the hotel.

Checkin:from 15:0023:59 hours

Checkout:until 12:00 hours

Impressive Punta Cana Hotel

Av. Alemania AB 108, Punta Cana, Dominican Republic

Set in Bavaro district, 2.2 km from Dolphin Island Park, Impressive Punta Cana Hotel features an infinity swimming pool and views of the garden. Wi Fi is available throughout the venue as well as a restaurant, live performances and a golf course are available on site.

This accommodation is in a 25minute walk from the vibrant Princess Tower Casino Punta Cana. The property is near by the beach. The modern Impressive Punta Cana Hotel is placed a few minutes' drive from Cortecito Beach.

432 beautiful rooms are fitted with ironing facilities, coffee and tea making facilities, and WiFi. The accommodation has elegant furniture and tiled flooring.

A buffet breakfast is provided for guests. The hotel has Open Sea International Buffet restaurant, which specialises in international cuisine. The bar's menu offers various types of soft drinks, beers and wines. A spa therapy and a fitness centre are included for free. Guests can work out at a pool area and relax in a sauna. Aerobics classes and fitness classes as well as darts, billiard and mini golf ensure active pastime.

Checkin:from 15:0023:30 hours

Checkout:until 12:00 hours

Sanctuary Cap Cana, AllInclusive Adult Resort

Playa Juanillo, Punta Cana, Dominican Republic
Featuring hire of boats and cars as well as WiFi throughout the property, Sanctuary Cap Cana,

AllInclusive Adult Resort is set in Punta Cana, 2.6 km from Playa Juanillo Beach. The venue is set about 17 minutes' walk from the sand beach.

This accommodation is also 3.7 km from Marina Cap Cana. The hotel places you within 1.4 km of Riu Republica. The upscale Jack Nicklaus Punta Espada Golf Club is only a few minutes' drive away.

The beautiful rooms at Sanctuary Cap Cana, AllInclusive Adult Resort feature a unique decor. Guests can enjoy views of the garden. Nice touches to enhance your stay include hairdryers, bath sheets and a tub.

A buffet breakfast is served in the mornings. Blue Marlin offers a seafood dinner. Poolside is the venue's own snack bar. Punta Cana airport is approximately 15 km away from the property.

Leisure options include a sunbathing terrace, a golf course and a nightclub along with chargeable facilities like loungers and a spa therapy. There is a private pool to enjoy your stay. The accommodation offers diving, ping pong and mountain biking for guests to practise sports.

Checkin:from 15:0019:00 hours

Checkout:until 08:0012:00 hours

Children and extra beds

There are no extra beds provided in a room.

There are no cots provided in a room.

Barcelo Bavaro Beach (Adults Only) Hotel Punta Cana

Carretera Bavaro Km 1, Punta Cana, Dominican Republic

Barcelo Bavaro Beach Hotel Punta Cana, located in Bavaro district, 4.7 km from Cortecito Beach, features views of the garden. There is a business centre and a photocopy machine at the resort.

Seaquarium Punta Cana Water Park is less than 2.1 km away. The venue places you within 0.2 km of El Cortecito. The own beach is 5 minutes' walk away. A short driving distance to Aroma's Museum is a perk for guests staying at Barcelo Bavaro Beach Hotel.

The accommodation features airconditioned rooms that come with cable TV with ondemand films, satellite TV and free WiFi. They are decorated with elegant furniture.

Start each day at the restaurant with buffet breakfast. Guests are invited to the onsite Caribe restaurant to indulge in culinary delights. The hotel's bar features a lounge, billiards and a spacious terrace. A game area, a community pool and a casino are available on the premises. There is a gym facility with a wide range of sports.

Checkin:from 15:0023:59 hours

Checkout:until 12:00 hours

Grand Palladium Punta Cana Resort & Spa

C/ El Cortecito, Playa Bavaro, Punta Cana, Dominican Republic

The exquisite Grand Palladium Punta Cana Resort & Spa is set 5 km from Manatee Park with easy access to restaurants, bars and golf courses. Some of 451 rooms offer views of the garden, while onsite there is a hot spring bath, a solarium and a wellness area.

The venue features accommodation in Bavaro district. A white beach is near by the hotel.

Cortecito Beach is also located near the property.

The unique units are fitted with WiFi, free wireless internet and cable channels. The rooms include a bathroom with a spa bathtub, a drier and a hair dryer.

You will find a buffet breakfast served at the restaurant. The à la carte restaurant offers you Indian dishes. A lobby bar features billiards table and a spacious terrace along with beers, soft drinks and tea. Sumptuori Restaurant and Helios Beach Club serve a selection of meals within 275 metres away. The venue provides aqua fitness and a wellness centre free of charge. Guests have free use of a gym and fitness centre. There is a fitness room with a wide range of sports.

Checkin:from 15:0023:59 hours

Checkout:until 12:00 hours

Majestic Elegance Punta Cana (Adults Only) Hotel

Cra El Macao, Arena Gorda, Punta Cana, Dominican Republic

The stylish Majestic Elegance Punta Cana Hotel is a great place to stay in Bavaro district in a reasonable distance from Arena Gorda Beach. Business travellers will appreciate conveniences like free WiFi in public areas and access to a photocopier, a desk and a business centre.

Cave Oleg Bat House is located 4.7 km from the venue and Punta Blanca Golf Club is just about 0.9 km away. The accommodation is placed not far from pristine beaches of Punta Cana.

Offering views of the ocean, the rooms come with multichannel television, complimentary WiFi and TV. They also have king fourposter beds and king size beds with feather pillows, down pillows and linens as well as marble flooring.

A buffet breakfast is provided daily. The hotel's pizza restaurant serves international cuisine. There is a cocktail bar where guests can enjoy wines, cocktails and soft drinks. Majestic Elegance Punta Cana Hotel is easily accessible from Punta Cana airport lying within 31 minutes' drive. With no extra pay, a spa therapy and yoga classes are offered. It boasts a range of facilities including a private swimming pool, a shared lounge and a bar, as well as fitness and a gym area for sport lovers. This residence has a gym.

Checkin:from 15:0023:59 hours

Checkout:until 12:00 hours

Dreams Punta Cana Hotel

Playas Uvero Alto, Punta Cana, Dominican Republic

Featuring a barber shop, a spa area and a solarium, Dreams Punta Cana Hotel offers accommodation in Punta Cana. El Merengue is 2.5 km from the resort and Carretera Uvero Alto Route is 1.5 km away.

The venue lies near the own beach. The hotel is located in Uvero Alto district. Sirenis Aquagames Punta Cana is only a short drive away.

The airy rooms at this venue have ironing facilities, satellite television and cable television. Guests can enjoy views of the ocean. A swimming pool provided on the a private balcony will add more comfort to your stay.

Start your day in the restaurant with a buffet breakfast. There is an à la carte restaurant and a swimup bar on site. Poolside has alcoholic drinks on offer. The menu of Amaya features Caribbean dishes. This property is approximately 45 km away from Punta Cana airport. Aqua fitness and a spa therapy can also be arranged for guests for free during their stay. After a tiring day you can relax in a wellness centre, a Jacuzzi and massage treatments. Dreams Punta Cana Hotel offers a variety of sport activities including diving, volleyball and sailing.

Checkin:from 15:0023:59 hours
Checkout:until 12:00 hours

Children and extra beds

There are no extra beds provided in a room.

Holiday homes

V&V Beach House

Calle Los Corales Residencial Los Corales, Punta Cana, Dominican Republic

Nice N Comfy Beach House Holiday home is located in Bavaro district of Punta Cana and features a sun terrace, a patio and a shared lounge. The venue is fitted with 2 bedrooms and 1 bathroom. Guests can enjoy an outdoor pool and prepare their own meals in a kitchenette.

Punta Cana airport is within a 20minute drive of the property while Plaza Bavaro is 1.7 km away. The villa is situated 15 minutes' walk of Palma Real Shopping Village. Offering a variety of dishes, Balicana Asian Cuisine, Gracehouse

Lounge Bar & Restaurant and Coyote Bar & Lounge are just about 150 metres away.Dolphin Island and Ocean Adventures Punta Cana are available within a few steps.

Rooms come with private bathrooms.

A kitchen is equipped with a fridge, a toaster and a cooktop.Guests can hire cars and bikes to explore the area.

Checkin:from 14:0015:00 hours

Checkout:until 11:0012:00 hours

Children and extra beds

There are no extra beds provided in a room.

There are no cots provided in a room.

Green Village 03 Punta Cana

Cap Cana Green Village, 3141, Punta Cana, Dominican Republic

Green ge 03 provides accommodation with an outdoor swimming pool, a patio and a tennis court in Cap Cana district of Punta Cana. It includes a minikitchen and 1 bathroom. This holiday home also features free WiFi throughout the venue.

Hoyo Azul is 3.1 km away, while Cap Cana is 1.8 km from the villa. The city centre is 9 km away. Green ge 03 is set a few minutes' drive from Juanillo Beach.

For your convenience, a hairdryer and bath sheets are provided in the bathroom, in addition to a sitting area, a dining area and ironing facilities in the rooms.

This property offers a microwave, coffee and tea making facilities, and a washing machine for guests' use. Punta Cana airport is a 19minute ride away. Green ge 03 features an own patio for guests' comfort. The outdoor activities include horseback riding and fishing.

Checkin:from 16:0023:59 hours

Checkout:until 10:00 hours

Children and extra beds

There are no extra beds provided in a room.

There are no cots provided in a room.

Hotel El Conde De Villa Rosa Punta Cana

Sector Villa Rosa, La Ceiba Del Salado, Veron Punta Cana, Punta Cana, Dominican Republic
Offering an aqua park, a patio and a shared lounge, Hotel El Conde De Villa Rosa is located 16 km from Arena Blanca Beach. It is composed of 2 bedrooms alongside with a kitchenette and 1 bathroom.

The property is 10 minutes' drive from Macao Beach.

Offering garden views, all units come with complimentary wireless internet, flatscreen TV and a dining area. A kitchen appointed with an electric kettle, a fridge and an oven as well as a private bathroom are at guests' disposal. There is a pillowtop mattress and feather pillows provided. You'll find nice touches like a hairdryer, complimentary toiletries and dressing gowns to enhance your stay.

The venue is about 35 minutes' drive from Punta Cana International airport.The property features a terrace with a shower.

Checkin:from 13:0022:00 hours
Checkout:until 10:0012:00 hours

Town House 36B, Punta Cana Village

36 Calle Cayena, Punta Cana, Dominican Republic

Set 3 km from the city centre, Town House 36B, Punta Cana Village offers free WiFi throughout the property. Free parking is provided on site.

Located 9 km off ChocoMuseo Punta Cana, the venue is 5 km from Punta Cana airport. Guests can easily reach La Cana Golf Club, which is about 3.1 km away.In the vicinity of the hotel there is Indigenous Eyes Ecological Reserve. Capilla Nuestra Senora de Punta Cana is a few minutes' walk away.

A TV set with satellite channels, a microwave and hifi are featured in all guest rooms at the property. All units will provide guests with dishwasher, coffee/tea makers and a washing machine.

Checkin:from 12:0022:00 hours

Checkout:until 11:00 hours

Children and extra beds

There are no extra beds provided in a room.

Punta Cana Family Home

Calle 4 Manzana 6 House Number 8 Ciudad La Palma, Punta Cana, Dominican Republic
Cielo Azul Village offers family accommodation

with an aqua park, a sun deck and a tennis court.

The building consists of 3 bedrooms and 2

bathrooms.

This Country house is 4.9 km from Bavaro

Adventure Park and 6 km from the city centre. La

Cana Golf Club is within 10 minutes' drive from

the venue.Cielo Azul Village is set in the vicinity

of Playa Juanillo.

A flatscreen TV with satellite channels, a heating system and a trouser press are available in each room. This property also has a kitchen and features garden views. Beds fitted with a down comforter and linens are at guests' disposal. For your comfort, you will find a hair dryer, a spa bathtub and a sink.

A microwave oven, dishwasher and coffee/tea making machines are provided for selfcatering.Windsurfing, diving and horse riding can be enjoyed onsite.

Checkin:from 15:0022:00 hours

Checkout:until 08:0011:00 hours

Children and extra beds

There are no cots provided in a room.

Costa Hermosa B102 Hotel Punta Cana

Punta Cana, Dominican Republic

The venue provides guests with free WiFi throughout the villa. At this property parking area is available nearby.

Set 7 km from Palma Real Shopping Village and 10 km from Manatee Park, the venue is located in Punta Cana. La Juntadera and Pastrata Mexican can be found 300 metres from the villa. Both Parroquia Jesus Maestro and Playa Juanillo are set just around the corner.

The accommodation includes climate control, television and ironing facilities in rooms.

A microwave, refrigerator and kitchenware are also provided. It is situated about 15 km from Punta Cana airport.

Checkin:from 16:0023:59 hours

Checkout:until 10:00 hours

Villa Diane Punta Cana

*Costa Bavaro, Villas Del Sol 2 Casa 132, Punta
Cana, Dominican Republic*
Situated in Bavaro district, Villa Diane features
airport shuttle bus service, laundry and
housekeeping service as well as a private
swimming pool. This Villa has 2 bedrooms and 2
bathrooms. Guests have access to free WiFi
throughout the venue.

It is located in a beach area, about 25 minutes'
walk from Yacht & catamaran sailing. Avalon
Casino Punta Cana is 3.8 km from the
accommodation.A short stroll will take you to
the Playa Juanillo.

Each room comes with an inroom safe, wireless
Internet and coffee/tea making facilities. Some
units also have a kitchen equipped with a
microwave, refrigerators and kitchenware. Beds

fitted with a pillowtop mattress and linens are available. A shower, a rollin shower and a bidet as well as bath robes, towels and slippers are included.

It is about a 20minute drive from Punta Cana airport.For sports, guests can enjoy diving, horseback riding and fisheries.

Checkin:from 14:0023:00 hours

Checkout:until 06:0010:00 hours

Children and extra beds

There are no cots provided in a room.

Corte Sea D302 Hotel Punta Cana

Punta Cana, Dominican Republic
At Corte Sea D302 villa you'll be in proximity to popular sights like Plaza Turquesa. Satellite TV, climate control and a patio are a standard in Corte Sea D302.

While staying at this venue, you'll be 3.6 km from Barcelo Golf Bavaro and 1.6 km from Dolphin Island Park. Gordito' s Fresh Mex and El Chiringuito are 300 metres from the accommodation. Corte Sea D302 is set a few minutes' drive from Iberostar Golf Course.

Additionally, you'll find a shower, a hairdryer and bath sheets.

A microwave, a refrigerator and kitchenware make dining convenient. The nearest airport is Punta Cana located within 15 km from Corte Sea D302.

Checkin:from 16:0023:59 hours

Checkout:until 10:00 hours

Children and extra beds

There are no extra beds provided in a room.

Villa Cocotal 206B Punta Cana

Punta Cana, Dominican Republic
Cocotal 206B offers an accommodation within 22 minutes by car from Punta Cana airport. A TV set with satellite channels, air conditioner and ironing facilities are available at the venue.

The villa is located in Punta Cana only 1.3 km from Palma Real Shopping Village. Mangu Disco is at 3.3 km distance away from the property. Guests will enjoy Caribbean meals in La Negra, which is 250 metres from the venue. Cocotal 206B is set a few minutes' drive from Dolphin Island Park.

Showers, hairdryers and a dryer are provided.

A microwave, a fridge and kitchenware are also at the guests' disposal.

Checkin:from 16:0023:59 hours

Checkout:until 10:00 hours

Bungalow In Cap Cana Caribbean Hotel Punta Cana

Green Village Cap Cana Cap Cana, Punta Cana, Dominican Republic

Offering a private pool, Bungalow In Cap Cana Caribbean is situated in Cap Cana district. Other facilities include a wellness area, complimentary parking and a Jacuzzi.

Hoyo Azul is located 3.3 km away from Bungalow In Cap Cana Caribbean. Punta Espada is within 1050 meters. Situated in Punta Cana, the villa is set close to Blue Hole.

Every unit comes with an inroom safe, a mini bar, heating, highvelocity internet and a dining area, and a kitchenette is included. Bathrooms come with a bath and a bidet.

A small fridge, coffee/tea making machines, a toaster and kitchenware are provided for selfcatering. Bungalow In Cap Cana Caribbean offers leisure options including an outdoor swimming pool and a golf course.

Checkin:from 09:0012:00 hours

Checkout:until 12:0014:00 hours

Children and extra beds

All children under the age of 16 may stay free of charge when using existing beds.

Economy hotels

Hotel Plaza Jireh Punta Cana

Carretera Veron Punta Cana, Punta Cana, Dominican Republic

Hotel Plaza Jireh Punta Cana, located 0.8 km from Centro de Internet, features free WiFi in the rooms. Guests who stay in the venue can park their car onsite.

Guests can have breakfast in the bar every morning.

Checkin:from 15:0023:59 hours

Checkout:until 12:00 hours

Children and extra beds

There are no extra beds provided in a room.

Coconuts Hotel Punta Cana

Calle Italia(Al Lado Del Casino Flamboyan) Plaza Ara, Punta Cana, Dominican Republic
Coconuts Hotel, located 6 km from Manati Park

Bavaro, features free WiFi throughout the venue.

The property comprises 36 rooms.

This Economy hotel offers accommodation in Bavaro district with nearby access to Avalon. Guests can quickly get to Dolphin Island Park, which is roughly 3.1 km away.Splash Water Park is also located near the venue. Nearby you will also find Palma Real Shopping Village.

A writing desk, a trouser press and a private toilet are standard in all rooms at the property.

The area features Coconut Coast Corral Smokehouse and Herman 311 within 100 metres of the hotel.

Checkin:from 08:0022:00 hours

Checkout:until 08:0010:00 hours

SunAdventureTravel Hotel Punta Cana

Avenida Barcelo Ifa Villas Bavaro, Punta Cana 23000 La Marina Cap Cana, Punta Cana, Dominican Republic

Featuring free WiFi throughout the property, SunAdventureTravel Hotel offers accommodation within 4.4 km from Princess Tower Casino Punta Cana. Manatee Park is less than 3.3 km away.

The venue is 650 metres from the sea in Punta Cana. The hotel is also about 23 km from Cap Cana Marina. Mangu Disco is only a short drive away.

The economy property offers rooms with a TV set with satellite channels, coffee and tea making equipment, and a seating area. They come with a drier and towels.

Guests can enjoy European and Italian meals at Restaurante Venezia within 10 minutes' walk of the venue.

Checkin:from 12:00 hours

Checkout:until 10:00 hours

Children and extra beds

All children under the age of 2 may stay at the price of us$ 15 per person per night in a cot.

All children under the age of 12 may stay at the price of us$ 20 per person per night in an extra bed.

Older children/adults may stay at the price of us$ 25 per person per night in an extra bed.

The End

Printed in Great Britain
by Amazon